JACQUELINE BAXTER

SCHOOL GOVERNANCE

Policy, Politics and Practices

POLICY PRESS SHORTS RESEARCH

First published in Great Britain in 2016 by

Policy Press
University of Bristol
1-9 Old Park Hill
Bristol
BS2 8BB
UK
t: +44 (0)117 954 5940
pp-info@bristol.ac.uk
www.policypress.co.uk

North America office:
Policy Press
c/o The University of Chicago Press
1427 East 60th Street
Chicago, IL 60637, USA
t: +1 773 702 7700
f: +1 773 702 9756
sales@press.uchicago.edu
www.press.uchicago.edu

British Library Cataloguing in Publication Data
A catalogue record for this book is available from the British Library.

Library of Congress Cataloging-in-Publication Data
A catalog record for this book has been requested.

ISBN 978-1-4473-2602-1 (hardcover)
ISBN 978-1-4473-2604-5 (ePub)
ISBN 978-1-4473-2605-2 (Mobi)

Cover design by Andrew Corbett
Printed and bound in Great Britain by CPI Group (UK) Ltd, Croydon, CR0 4YY
Policy Press uses environmentally responsible print partners

To Robert, Alex, Harry and William Bellew,
who supported me through many hours spent
'governing', and to the school staff, governors and
students that made the experience so rewarding.

Contents

Foreword

For many years now, there has been a strong focus in education on the leadership and management of institutions. Matters of governance have been relatively neglected. Some years ago, I wrote that generalisations were frequently made about the features associated with effective school leadership, with little or no account being taken of the specific and diverse frameworks of policy and governance within which that leadership was exercised.

That narrow approach has proved increasingly unsustainable in the light of the transformative changes that policymakers have imposed on school systems in many countries, perhaps most notably in England. The concept of governance is not just about the steering of individual institutions, but refers to the entire set of arrangements under which a school system is organised and regulated. An important feature of this valuable and insightful book is that, drawing on a wide range of literature, it places school governing in a broad political and social context.

The position of school governing bodies in the English system has long been ambiguous. They have few parallels in other countries and are an expression of a cultural commitment to the idea of a school as a distinct and separate entity rather than as a part of a national system. From the 1970s onwards, this historic legacy was given a more modern, democratic aspect by including on governing bodies representatives of staff, parents, local employers, students and the wider community – the so-called 'stakeholder' model.

This model has come under pressure from the increasing devolution of responsibilities to schools and, in particular, the growing policy emphasis upon the idea of the 'independent state school'. This was heavily promoted by former Labour Prime Minister Tony Blair and was based on his experience of, and evident attachment to, the uniquely British model of the fee-charging independent or 'public' school, a prestigious institution running itself with minimal regulation and responsible mainly to its own governing body, its survival determined by its success in recruiting the children of wealthy parents. He assumed that these features could readily and successfully be transferred to the very much larger publicly funded sector, with its much wider set of accountabilities. Michael Gove, Conservative Education Secretary in the Coalition government that took office in 2010, later seized on Blair's initiative and aimed to expand it dramatically via a huge growth of the academies programme that had been initiated by Blair's government. Local oversight was largely removed from schools that became academies, although central oversight increased, and more freedom was granted to them over curriculum, finance, premises and the management of staff.

As this volume amply documents, this shift has put enormous strain on the very large unpaid force of volunteer school governors. An 'independent state school' arguably implies a board of directors with a broad range of skills that is unlikely to be found within the stakeholder model, or perhaps at all for more than a relatively small proportion of the large number – 20,000 plus – of schools in widely different contexts to which it is ultimately intended to apply. The book describes the slow attrition of the stakeholder model and the attempt, which may be doomed to failure, to replace it by a model in which governors are appointed largely for their professional skills and abilities, operating almost as a middle tier in what has become a highly centralised system of control.

The complexity does not end there. Many schools that were hitherto separate entities have formed themselves, or have been formed by government diktat if they were perceived to be failing, into formal groupings of various kinds: chains, alliances, federations, clusters. Paradoxically, this represents an unprecedented movement in the opposite direction from the historic English emphasis on school separatism and suggests that there exists a degree of antipathy towards, and even a fear of, the full working-out of the independent state school notion. In many of these arrangements, the governing body at the individual school level is purely advisory, and in some, it may not exist at all.

Jacqueline Baxter concludes her study by saying that school governors are central to our system. They are indeed. They have been given a central role in the new framework designed by the policymakers, and whether it succeeds or fails is likely, at least in part, to turn on the ability of governing bodies to sustain it.

I have been a member of three school governing bodies and am currently a trustee of one of the new cooperative school groupings. I believe that this absorbing book will enable all those with any involvement in this area to gain an invaluable depth of understanding of the forces shaping the complex and challenging new world of school governance.

Ron Glatter
Emeritus Professor of Educational Administration and Management,
The Open University

Visiting Professor, University College London (UCL)
Institute of Education

Honorary President, British Educational Leadership, Management and
Administration Society (BELMAS)

Preface

In the same way that Deem, Brehony and Heath's (1995) study of active citizenship and the governing of schools between 1988 and 1992 began with their own experiences as school governors, my interest in the subject initially derived from the 18 years I served as a school governor in Bedfordshire, England, four of which I also spent as a parent governor representative on Bedfordshire County Council's Select Committee for Lifelong Learning.

I began my tenure as a school governor in 1994 in a tiny village primary school in Cople. With only 70 pupils, the school was the hub of village life – an integral part of the community. At the time, my first child had just started school, and having come from a career in the City, I had no notion of what it meant to be a school governor. As in the case of many governors, it was not until another parent, a long-standing governor, approached me and sounded me out that I gave it any thought at all. Even though that was over 20 years ago, I still remember what she said to me: "We need people like you on the governing body, why don't you give it a try."

I still ponder over that statement – what kind of qualities did she think I had that would make me effective in the role? Was it that I was a parent with three small children, all of whom would eventually pass through the school gates? Was it my business background and pre-children career that made me an attractive proposition? Or was it that I had just embarked on a teaching course and knew something (very little) about education? Then I found out that I would have to stand for election – that this was not a done deal – and the whole prospect became even more unnerving. When I asked what the role would involve, the response was equally opaque: "You just come along to meetings, discuss stuff, that sort of thing; you'll enjoy it, really you will."

So, 20-something years on from that first encounter at the school gates, has anything changed with regard to becoming a school governor? Somewhat surprisingly, my research for this book with governors and their families has revealed that despite much work done by a whole raft of organisations dedicated to the recruitment of and support for school governors, very little has changed. It would appear that before taking up their role, many governors were as ignorant of what that role would involve as I was back in 1994. Furthermore, like me, many of them struggled to understand their function once in post.

This book draws on the many books written and on much of the good work undertaken on school governing by academics, practitioners and those that support them. In so doing, it attempts to place school governing in a wider context, looking at its role not purely in terms of education, but also in terms of wider political, cultural and social influences – its context as both volunteer occupation and educational function.

It also draws on my own research over the last four years on governance and governing and I am heavily indebted to governors and governor support organisations for the insights that they have given into this complex and multifaceted role. I would like to offer particular thanks to the National Governors' Association (NGA), the Key for School Governors and Modern Governor, as well as the many practitioners and policymakers that have engaged in lively debate on Twitter and in other forums.

I would also like to thank the schools and national and local organisations that helped to coordinate interviews and talks with governors.

Thanks must also go: to the journalists who agreed to be interviewed, whose unique perspective has contributed a great deal to the research and to my understanding of the workings of the media; and to the professional identities research group at the Open

University and to the British Educational Leadership, Management and Administration Society (BELMAS) Special Interest Group on Governance and Governing, whose insights and knowledge in the field of governing have contributed rich multidimensional perspectives to my knowledge on school governors and their role. I am particularly grateful to colleagues at the Key for School Governors association, particularly Fergal Roche and Nathan Easy, for data that contributed to Chapter Five, and to Emma Knights, CEO of the National Governors' Association (NGA), for her thoughtful comments and national overview of school governing, which have greatly contributed to the book. Thanks also go to Sue Littlemore of the Education Media Centre, for her insights into using education research in media reports, and to Baroness Estelle Morris, Patron of the Education Media Centre, for giving up her time to talk to me about her understandings of the complex relationship between education policy and the media.

Finally, I am most grateful to the Centre for Citizenship, Identities and Governance (CCIG) at the Open University, which funded much of this research, to academics based at the centre, in particular, Emeritus Professor John Clarke, for the support I received and to the reviewers who gave up time to review and comment on the draft proposal and manuscript.

Jacqueline Baxter
2015

Good questions outrank easy answers.
(Paul Samuelson)

INTRODUCTION

Aims and approach

In March 2014, an anonymous document arrived on the desk of the leader of Birmingham City Council. The document, sent with a covering letter – also anonymous – claimed that a number of schools in Birmingham had been deliberately targeted by hard-line Muslim school governors (Clarke, 2014; DfE, 2014c). The accusations within the letter alleged that these governors were 'plotting' to replace school leaders in several schools with individuals who were imposing a hard-line Muslim curriculum (Gov.uk, 2015).

Although the letter turned out to be a hoax, the affair, and the media storm that followed (Adams, 2014; Baxter, 2014b; BBC, 2014), uncovered a number of 'concerns' that had been expressed, both in the media and elsewhere, about the rapid changes taking place within education since the general election of 2010 and the coming to power of a Conservative–Liberal Democratic Coalition government (James et al, 2011; Wilkins, 2014). These issues were bound up with deep and prevailing concerns around the whole area of English education and the apparent erosion of a democratic and equitable system of education for all (see Scheurich and Skrla, 2004; Sun et al, 2007; Ball, 2009; Ozga et al, 2013).

These were not new concerns, but, in essence, reflect those raised in a growing body of academic literature that has been building since the Education Reform Act 1988 introduced the idea of independent state schools. The introduction of 'local management of schools', as it was termed, heralded the beginning of 'school autonomies' in England, allowing schools to 'break free' of local authority budgetary control (see Maclure, 1989; Sharp, 2002). These changes intensified under New Labour's academies project (1997–2010) and subsequent Education Acts (Education (Schools) Act 1992, Education Act 2005, Academies Act 2010, Education Act 2011), and have radically changed the structure of the English education system, permitting further financial and curricular autonomies, and introducing free schools and encouraging collaborations between schools (academy chains, multi-academy trusts and cooperative and maintained groups of federated schools). In England, these changes have created a marketised environment in which schools compete for pupils, which rather than creating educational equity, has compromised it (see Hatcher, 1994, 2006; Hatcher and Jones, 2011): a system that some have termed 'a systemless system' (Lawn, 2013; Lawn et al, 2014).

One of the main concerns – which, at the time of writing, remains unresolved – has been how, in a system that is now made up of so many different types of schools, the system of educational democratic accountability that had evolved since the Second World War can continue to operate effectively given the sweeping changes that have so completely altered its make-up (Ofsted, 2004; Ozga et al, 2013; Parliament, 2013a).

A second but no less pressing concern has been how the 300,000 volunteer school governors tasked with the strategic management of schools are coping with the new autonomies, financial freedoms and lack of local authority support that have taken place as a result of these changes (see Parliament, 2013a, 2013b, 2013c), for at the same time as schools are being offered freedom from local authority control – by becoming or being made to become academies – the power, reach and budgets of local authorities have been subject to dramatic cuts (see Sharp, 2002). These cuts have been so wide-ranging that, in some areas, education departments have ceased to exist, and many schools are left with no other option but to buy in services that were traditionally provided by the local education authority (LEA) (for more information, see Chapters Four and Five). Educationally, these trends have also left a yawning gap in the local knowledge base, as long-standing, highly experienced staff have been lost in the maelstrom (Sharp, 2002).

Although the Trojan Horse affair, as it became known, undoubtedly placed school governing well and truly in the media eye, it was not solely responsible for today's focus on school governing, but rather represents part of a trend that has intensified over the course of the last five years – a trend that has manifested in a number of ways, not least a dramatic increase in levels of scrutiny by the Office for Standards in Education, Children's Services and Skills (Ofsted), as well as a number of parliamentary inquiries (Parliament, 2013a, 2013b, 2013c). Alongside these rising levels of interest, the media have become increasingly 'sensitised' to issues around school governing, picking up far more stories about school governors and their work. The processes via which this sensitisation has been effected are discussed more fully in Chapter Three.

The interest shown by the government, media and inspectorate has put school governing on the national political agenda in a way that it has not experienced before. Discourses of the 'professional governor' abound as increasing pressure is placed on recruiting governors who come 'ready-made' to take on a raft of financial and managerial responsibilities (Wilkins, 2014). Yet, this in itself is causing considerable issues in governor recruitment, particularly in deprived areas, which have traditionally struggled to recruit high-quality governors.

This book employs a particular case, the Trojan Horse affair, in order to investigate what it has revealed about the current state of education governance in England. As such, the case functions as 'a defining moment' set against the backdrop of social, educational, economic and political changes leading up to and following the affair. Looking back over the period 2010 to 2015, a time of sweeping changes within the public services, this book examines how political and cultural factors have affected the governance of schools in England

Education in the UK is devolved. However, the book is set within the English context because although the other home nations within the UK have similar school governing arrangements, they have not been subjected to such sweeping educational reforms as those experienced in England.

I hope that the in-depth research into school governing and its contextualisation within the framework of public service governance will prove interesting not only to scholars working in the areas of education, the voluntary sector and public services, but equally to school governors themselves and those who work alongside them.

Education as a public service

Accountability and the quality of UK public services have preoccupied both public and government ever since William Beveridge (1942) identified the five 'giant evils' of squalor, ignorance, want, idleness and disease that plagued society, and proposed the sweeping transformation of the welfare system that took place after the Second World War. Since then, many UK general elections have been lost and won according to which party is considered to be better at maintaining the precarious balance between keeping taxes as low as possible and providing public services fit for use (Boix, 1998). Indeed, since 1945, few UK governments can be said to have achieved this balance – despite specious claims to the contrary (Burton, 2014).

It is sometimes forgotten that education – perceived as the cornerstone of a democratic society and viewed today as fundamental to economic competitiveness – was one of the core elements within the Beveridge reform (Lawton, 1979), and even that it is a core area of social policy (see Finch, 1984). However, in common with other areas of public services, the difficulties of retaining a democratic and equitable education system exercise government no less now than they did in that seemingly distant post-war period (Maclure, 1989).

If ensuring the provision of fair and equitable public services is testing, then ensuring democratic accountability provides an equal if not greater challenge, particularly during times of austerity, when cuts across public services make attaining even baseline levels of quality a challenge (Blyth, 2013).

Governing, governance and school governing in a democratic system

In order to understand where school governing fits within the broader areas of 'governing' and 'governance', I begin by defining the latter terms and the ways in which they are used in this book and then turn to the ways that school governance is positioned within the democratic system of governance that operates within the UK.

From governing to governance

'Governance' is not an easy term to define and, as Newman (2001, p 12) points out, it has 'become a rather promiscuous concept, linked to a wide range of theoretical perspectives and policy approaches'. In its most simplified form (for it is far from being simple), it refers to the 'new theories and practices of governing and the dilemmas to which they give rise' (Bevir, 2013, p 1). It attempts to describe a very 'particular set of changes, a deeply significant set of shifts in the way that government seeks to govern' (Pierre and Peters, 2000, in Newman, 2001, p 11). Essentially, it marks the changes that have occurred between the state and society over the last century; changes that have taken place within the context of global social and economic shifts. These shifts have also been characterised through a shift in power, 'away from traditional government institutions, upwards to transnational bodies and downwards to regions and sub-regions' (Newman, 2001, p 11).

Newman's (2001, p 33) work on New Labour's (1997–2010) models of governance outlines some of the tensions between centralised and decentralised approaches to governing, outlining the departures from old bureaucratic hierarchical models of governance that were (and still are) predicated on the power of the bureau. These old models are characterised by 'slow changes, are brought about primarily via alterations in legislation, standards and procedures, cascading down vertical hierarchies of the governance system' (Newman, 2001, p 33). In contrast, governance from New Labour to the present Conservative administration aligns more closely with what Newman describes as the rational goal model, which is a model characterised by the dispersal of power across:

> a wide range of agencies rather than concentrated in monolithic hierarchies, with an emphasis on managerial rather than bureaucratic power: with rewards and penalties for the delivery of government targets and policy goals, and accountability via a number of none or quasi-governmental organisations. (Newman, 2001, p 34)

Kooiman (2003, p 4, emphases added) offers a useful distinction for thinking about the differences between 'governing' and 'governance', stating that 'governing can be considered as the *totality of interactions* in which public as well as private actors participate' – activities 'aimed at solving societal problems or creating societal opportunities' – while 'governance' may be understood as 'the *totality of theoretical conceptions* on governing'. This definition has been used by a number of researchers as a foundation for researching the complex relationship between the state, market and civil society (see, eg, Clarke, 2007; Newman and Clarke, 2009).

Governance assumes even greater complexity given that society is largely planned by politicians or the activities of public administration, whose 'interpretations of policy objectives are brought into the realm of values, choices and actions' (Stenvall, 1993, p 62). These choices in policymaking are often less influenced by 'evidence', relying more on the 'world view', or ideology of the ruling party (Stenvall, 1993, p 64). These ideologies and world views are often highly influential in the ways that governments conceptualise the world and the role of the public services within that world. These beliefs and ideologies are not confined to national governments, but often replicated on a global scale, influenced by transnational organisations such as the World Bank (Klees et al, 2012). In terms of education, the proliferation of such international agencies has greatly influenced national policies and governments' particular ways of thinking about the role and function of education (Ozga et al, 2013).

Economic ideas and political thought more broadly have evolved in response to national and international economic and societal drivers occurring since 1945, and these factors have also exerted a profound effect on the organisations and agencies involved in the governance process (see, eg, King, 1987; Crouch, 2003). In the UK, public services have radically altered since the end of the post-war welfare consensus – the period immediately following the Second World War when the Labour and Conservative Parties put aside their differences to focus on rebuilding Britain – adopting a more marketised approach, marked by the election of a Conservative government under Margaret Thatcher in 1979, and undergoing a shift in understandings of what it means to be a citizen within a democratic system of government (King, 1987). Citizens have also been subject to tensions because of these changes as they are positioned by economic, political and social factors outside of their control (Marshall, 1964). As part of government projects aimed at creating economic, social and political stability, all manner of rights have been subject to evaluation and re-evaluation:

> Civil rights: freedom of speech, the right to own property, equality before the law; political rights and rights associated with participation, along with social rights: economic and welfare rights guarantees of a certain educational level, economic security, public welfare and heath provision. (Marshall, in King, 1987, p 33)

The global rise of New Right ideals (economic and political liberalism), largely in response to the oil crisis of the 1970s and instigated, in part, through the failure of Keynesian economic policy, assumed global momentum as economies struggled to make economic sense of a period marked by 'high unemployment and rapid inflation' (King, 1987, p 3). These ideals supported shrinking the welfare state and reducing the role of government in every area of public life. This way of thinking, with its emphasis on individualism, choice and the ability of the citizen to 'take responsibility' for their actions and choices, assumes that individuals will pursue wealth and that, in so doing, this self-interest will 'generate a collective prosperity which could not be so effective if planned by an external agent' (such as the government) (King, 1987, p 10). This world view assumes a very different view of the public servant to the dominant, value-driven view of public servants during the period of the post-war consensus. In contrast, in the more marketised environment of the late 1970s onwards, public servants were looked upon with increasing suspicion: the public servant, 'in the absence of profit driven behaviours, was assumed to be primarily motivated by: salary, public reputation, power, patronage, ease of management and ease of making changes' (King, 1987, p 10). These were not traits that were thought to align with responsive and cost-effective public services, and this mode of thinking not only created high levels of government mistrust of public servants, but equally contributed to target-driven , 'command and control' policy approaches, such as those seen during the New Labour administration, when the Prime Minister's Delivery Unit led by Sir Michael Barber implemented a raft of target-driven reforms to education, health, crime and transport (Barber, 2008). In terms of education, the belief that this approach works well is highly contested, and target-driven reforms are thought by many researchers to have produced a system that is largely evaluated by statistical data, which, in many cases, hides or obfuscates context and other important considerations (see, eg, Seddon, 2008; Ozga et al, 2011).

Newman's (2001, p 11) commentary on the flow of power away from traditional government institutions, upwards to transnational bodies and downwards to regions and sub-regions, is useful in the particular case of education, the policies of which have been heavily influenced by transnational organisations such as the Organisation for Economic Co-operation and Development (OECD), whose international comparators have increasingly exerted powerful influences on policy at the national level (OECD, 2010a, 2011). As Chapter Three details, reports from these institutions – such as the Programme for International Student Assessment (PISA) – have exerted considerable influence on policy via the media, who, in turn, have embraced the apparently 'uncomplicated' and 'storified' manner in which comparison data is displayed (Baxter and Rönnberg, 2014). The newsworthiness of these reports has not diminished, despite criticisms around the comparability of the data that have been pointed out by a number of researchers in the field (see Grek, 2009).

In the UK, the notion of 'choice' has been central to the governance of public services since the 'intersection of two ideologies: those of the New Right and those of managerialism' (Clarke and Newman, 1997, p 34). Clarke and Newman argue that it is the beliefs of those that embrace the collective set of ideas that go to make up New Right ideology that have driven the 'ideals' of 'choice' and education (and all public services) as a market. These ideals have been subject to a great deal of scrutiny in the field of education and the findings are far from conclusive in terms of whether parents really do have a choice or whether the term is misleading and 'choice' is dependent on earning power and social class, which only applies to 'certain parents' (see Ball, 1993; Glatter et al, 1997; Gorard, 1999; Bagley et al, 1996, 2001).

School governance and school governors within a system of democratic governance

Drawing on the dynamic changes that have occurred within the structures and organisation of governing, school governance can be viewed from a political perspective in which it is central to the governance of education. As part of one of a number of different organisations that govern education, and in common with other organisations of this nature, it is a 'site of conflict, alliances, negations and accommodations' (Newman, 2001, p 173).

Within this system, school governors function as part of a system of 'checks and balances' that combines regulatory oversight with ideas of democratic participation (Clarke, 2009). Deem and colleagues, writing in 1995, saw school governance as a key site of tension between the principles of the market and the democratic ideals of the representation of citizens in a democracy: 'Seen as acting as, and in part see[ing] themselves as, regulatory agents, engaged in surveillance over teachers and head teachers ... regarded as guardians of efficiency and effectiveness' (Deem et al, 1995, p 27).

This seemingly paradoxical interweaving of market principles and democratic ideals has characterised governance and governing since the late 1980s and forms part of the wide literature around what is seen to be a 'democratic deficit' in post-war Western democracies (see, eg, Wells et al, 2002; Mair, 2013). This 'democratic deficit' is articulated by a lack of public engagement not only in politics, but more widely across every area of public life (see, eg, Rayner, 2003). In the case of the UK, the anti-political/anti-engagement sentiments of the 1990s, which are seen to have contributed to the deficit, are well summed up by this quote from Labour Prime Minister Tony Blair in Mair's (2013) book *Ruling the void: The hollowing out of Western democracy*:

> For him [Blair] the new 'progressive' agenda was not to provide solutions from above, but to help citizens to search for their own solutions – 'to help people make the most of themselves.' Politics in this sense was not about exercising the 'directive hand' of government, but about the synergy that could be generated by combining 'dynamic markets' with 'strong communities.' (Mair, 2013, p 4)

Today's governors function within the UK system of democratic governance as 'semi-independent or parastatal actors', permitting government to 'address a wide range of social issues simultaneously without having to be involved with the minutiae of day-to-day socio-political interactions' (Flinders, 2008, p 3; see also Durose et al, 2009). Public disillusionment (and disaffection) with government has led to the proliferation of organisations, agencies and individuals who facilitate forms of governance that are superficially 'depoliticised' – 'free from political influence' – a phenomenon that has become known as 'governing at arm's length' (Clarke, 2011). As such, these organisations act as a 'constitutional brace to help rebuild public confidence [in government and the state]' (Flinders, 2008, p 12). Within this model of governance, school governors, in their democratic representative and custodian role, also function as the link between the state and the citizen.

The positioning of governors as both democratic representatives and custodians/managers responsible for the strategic imagining and monitoring of school improvement is also part of a wider tension within the post-welfare society, a tension born from the government tendency to view citizens as consumers. As John Clarke and colleagues point out:

> This new articulation … of citizen consumer involved a particular positioning of government as mediator in a relationship between the public and public services. Increasingly, the reform of public service provision had placed service providers at 'arms-length' from government. Marketisation, devolution, decentralisation and the construction of agencies responsible for delivery … were distinctive features in the emergent new governance of public services. (Clarke and Newman, 1997, in Clarke et al, 2007, p 31)

During an earlier study into school governance, Ranson et al (2005, p 356) described 'the creation of over 400,000 volunteer citizens between 1986–1988 … to occupy reformed school governing bodies and school boards[1] across the UK', as the 'largest democratic experiment in voluntary public participation'. Their study also makes the important point that although:

> the public spaces of school governance as 'intermediary associations' exemplify the potential for reconstituting civil society in its local and cultural variety … the state has also perceived school governance as a space to regulate universal improvement of educational standards and thus steer the modernization of a key public service. (Ranson et al, 2005, p 359)

Under the 2015 framework for school inspection (Ofsted, 2015), this body of individuals not only act as a link between the state and the citizen, but also as middle-tier regulators for their schools or groups/

chains of schools – they, in turn, are regulated by Ofsted and a new system of school commissioners (see Chapters Four and Five).

Democratic theory situates citizens in a number of roles:

> at one extreme is the classical ideal of active citizens, who directly participate in public decisions in a face-to face context alongside their peers; at the other end of the spectrum is the Schumpeterian elitist conception, whereby relatively passive individuals choose between different elites that compete with the vote leaving experts in charge of day to day affairs between elections. (John, 2009, p 13)

The extent to which the move to 'consumerise' the citizen has curtailed democratic participation in public services is contested: some writers argue that market reforms have created a far greater input from the public into how services are run, effectively offering them more power in services (King, 1987); others argue that, in reducing service users to 'consumers', the reforms have residualised concerns over contextual inequalities in service levels (Clarke et al, 2007).

The Conservative public service reforms of the 1980s that contributed to this consumerisation of citizens were justified on the premise that they would create 'better public services': more responsive to service users (ergo customers); more agile in terms of responding to changes in the 'market'; and more able to respond to service user needs. In order to achieve this, the Conservative government under John Major introduced a number of measures under the umbrella of the Citizens' Charter; these measures were designed to offer citizens more say in the ways in which public services were run (Major, 1991, 2000). In effect, this meant that organisations were urged to become more 'transparent' and led to the introduction of targets and performance goals in order to facilitate this 'transparency' and to permit service users to make comparisons in service levels between organisations. This resulted in the publication of the performance data of public service organisations, which aimed to give citizens more 'choice' in terms of their service provider (Clarke et al, 2007).

Outline of the book

The challenges posed by political, economic and social changes since the Second World War have affected governing, governance and school governors. This book begins with a brief outline in Chapter One of the role that school governors play in educational governance in England, describing the challenges that they face and those that led up to the Trojan Horse affair in 2014. In so doing, it illustrates the ways in which unprecedented levels of reform led up to the affair, and the catalytic effect that it has had on policy since then. It also highlights the myriad ways in which the politicisation of education has encroached upon the whole area of compulsory education in England and how this, in turn, has impacted on democratic governance and accountability.

Chapter Two details the unravelling of the Trojan Horse affair and the ways in which it revealed that the government's peremptory and Panglossian ideal of an 'excellent education system', as articulated via the academies project, has, to a great extent, overlooked the vital area of education governance. The affair has not only revealed a troubling set of issues related to governance, but by manifesting as a 'media storm', 'an Islamist plot' and the apotheosis of an 'ideological drive' by a senior government minister, has also become a watershed for future policy and practices in this area. Chapter Two offers a detailed description of the affair and examines it in terms of both its media impact and the issues that it raises around school governance, which are then explored throughout ChaptersThree, Four and Five. Introducing the affair, the book examines to what extent it was crafted by the media and how it was used and manipulated to create a discourse that was subsequently employed as a policy driver. It also outlines its origins, examining the language and the ways in which the affair was crafted and framed in order to create intense public interest. As explained earlier, the Trojan Horse affair did not occur in isolation, but in common with many such 'defining episodes' manifested as the culmination of a number of factors: contextual, cultural and political. One of the defining factors of the event was the way in which it was used to create a discourse – 'a set of ideas, concepts and categorizations' (Hajer, 1993, p 44) – which were subsequently employed in order to justify changes to policy and practice. These aspects begin to be explored in Chapter Two and continue in Chapter Three, which explores, through a press analysis, how similar 'media tropes' have been crafted by the press and media and the particular ways in which they influenced public opinion in other areas of public policy. Chapter Four also helps to explain the ways in which an affair that was essentially a failure of governance became conflated with Islamism, extremism and the threat of terrorism. In placing the affair within the context of what is known as the 'mediatisation of education policy' – a field of research that explores and examines the complex ways in which the media influences and shapes policy – it looks back on the ways in which school governing has been framed in the media, beginning with the period 2008–09 just before the election of Conservative–Liberal Democrat Coalition government and ending with the period just prior to the Trojan Horse affair in 2014, examining how, within the space of just seven years, school governors and governance came to be re-imagined by the press and media.

Chapter Five examines another area that was highlighted by the affair: democratic accountability. Beginning with an overview of democratic accountability in the public services in the run-up to the general election in 2010, the chapter moves on to discuss the changing role of the service user, parent, patient and public before moving on to educational accountability and the role of school governance from 1990 to 2015. In so doing, it explores the effects of New Public Management and the impact of inspection regimes on education. Following on from this, the concluding sections move to discussing the changing accountabilities within the education system from 2010 to 2015 and the ways in which governors featured within them, exploring the implications for the Conservative government elected in May 2015.

Chapter Six builds on the previous chapters by exploring how governors themselves are experiencing the changing nature of school governance, examining how particular governing bodies, working within new structures in particularly challenging contexts, are making sense of their environment and role during this period of rapid educational change. Drawing on a case study of governors in multi-academy trusts (MATs) situated in demanding areas of high deprivation, the study examines why these individuals became school governors, exploring what they see as being the particular challenges and rewarding aspects of their role. Using qualitative interview data and drawing on theories of organisational sense-making, the chapter examines how new roles and responsibilities combine with the challenges of governing in tough areas and, as a consequence, impact on the way governors think about their role/s.

The final chapter of the book – Chapter Seven – examines the policy changes that have occurred since the Trojan Horse event, exploring these in light of the election of a Conservative government under David Cameron in May 2015. The chapter also looks at how policy and public thinking have been influenced not only by the affair itself, but also by the affair as placed in the wider context of international terrorist threats such as the rise of Islamic State.[2] It also looks to the ways in which a heightened emphasis on promoting 'British values' has affected the governor role.

Research methodology and data

The study draws on 60 qualitative interviews with school governors and 15 interviews with journalists, alongside interviews with policymakers and a number of interviews with other stakeholders in school governing. Each interview lasted approximately 30–45 minutes and were carried out over the period from January 2013 to December 2015 as part of an Open University Project, 'Governing Their Future'. The project continues to investigate governor identities and perceptions of the role at a time of intense and substantial changes to English education and explores key influences on the role of school governors, including: press and media; training/development; and regulation and inspection. More specifically, Chapter Six draws on face-to-face interviews with governors from two particular MATs set in areas of high deprivation. A total of 22 self-selecting governors were interviewed for this study, with interviews lasting approximately 45 minutes each.

Chapters Two and Three also include interviews with 15 journalists and editors, each one either a current or past education correspondent. The project also draws on substantial documentary evidence, including: academic papers; government documents; Select Committee Transcripts of Evidence; newspaper reports (from the Lexis Nexis database); and information from governor support and recruitment websites, for example, the National Governors' Association and the Key for School Governors association.

Chapter Five also draws on inspection reports, documentation and data from a previous project, 'Governing by Inspection', led by Professor Jenny Ozga of the University of Oxford and funded by the Economic and Social Research Council (ESRC) (grant number: RES-062-23-2241-A), as well as more recent inspection reports, data from the Ofsted website and academic reports on inspection and regulation. The chapter also draws on data from the OECD on inspection and regulation and benefits from rich insights gained from colleagues on the 'Governing by Inspection' project and from Melanie Ehren and colleagues presenting at the University of Gothenburg Inspection Symposium, 'The Changing Face of School Inspections: Theories and Practices'.

Notes

[1] 'School governing bodies' and 'school boards' are historically used interchangeably in research pertaining to school governing. However, the term 'school board' is increasingly used when speaking about academies and free schools, whereas 'governing body' is still predominantly employed when referring to state-maintained schools. In this book, these terms are used interchangeably in order to talk about schools more broadly rather than distinguish between academies, free schools and state-maintained schools.

[2] There are at least four alternative names and abbreviations for the group: Islamic State (IS), Islamic State of Iraq and Syria (ISIS), Islamic State of Iraq and the Levant (Isil), or Daesh – which is based on a derogatory Arabic acronym. In this book we use 'Islamic State' or 'ISIS'.

ONE

SCHOOL GOVERNING:
A MOMENT IN TIME

Volunteering in changing political contexts

School governors make up one of the largest volunteer bodies in the country, a body that has been referred to as the 'biggest experiment in democratic governance ever undertaken' (Ranson et al, 2005, p 225). There are no official statistics relating to how many school governors there are, their gender or their ethnicity; at the time of writing, there is no official national register. Based on the number of schools in England, numbers have unofficially been estimated at around 300,000.

In many ways, school governing is a unique type of volunteering – often not being thought of as such, even by governors themselves. As one governor put it:

> "It's funny actually, because I've never really considered being a governor as volunteering – I saw something a few years ago about volunteering and thought, 'Oh, people should volunteer more'. I thought, 'Yeah, I ought to volunteer more', and then I thought, 'Actually, I'm a governor'." (Primary governor, May 2015)

Yet, volunteering it is, being subject to the same political and cultural influences as any other type of volunteering work, and the part that it plays in society is largely conditioned by government attitudes, policies and ideologies.

The number of people across Europe who volunteer is surprisingly large. A European Union (EU) study carried out in 2010 revealed that 92 million to 94 million people (22% to 23%) over the age of 15 living in the EU were involved in volunteering (GHK, 2010). The same study indicated that in most European countries, the number of active volunteers had increased since 2000.

Voluntary work is of considerable importance, not least because of its impact on and benefits for local communities, society in general and, of course, the volunteers themselves. It is also of considerable importance to government and is, in many ways, subject to the same vacillations and vagaries of government policy as those that prevail across the employment market. It should come as no surprise that the attitude of government towards volunteering and the part that it plays in a government's vision of society has been shown to exert substantial influence on the ways in which the public themselves perceive volunteering, while also exerting a profound effect on the number of individuals putting themselves forward for voluntary work.

Volunteering, 1960–2010

In England, trends in volunteering have ebbed and flowed. By 1960, the:

> glory days of the welfare state were over. It had become clear that demand for public services would always exceed supply, costs were at the limits of affordability and, in any case, there were cracks, gaps and bumps in existing provision. (Rochester et al, 2012, p 86)

What is more, the government was tiring of the difficulties of managing professionals, finding their attitude to change obstructive and their manner of closing rank against government irksome. A Home Office document published in 1967 remarks upon the 'spontaneity, adaptability and freshness of approach' of volunteers (Home Office, 1967, p 3, cited in Rochester et al, 2012, p 86). This approach also combined with a prevailing view among government that 'volunteers were essential to a democratic society and worthy of "admiration and respect in their own right"' (Home Office, 1978, p 31, cited in Rochester et al, 2012, p 86). As a consequence of these sentiments, government attitudes to volunteering in the public services took a big step forward when a report by the Seebohm Committee in 1968 proposed a 'Radical re-engineering of local authorities' delivery of community based social services' (cited in Rochester et al, 2012, p 33).

Volunteers were to play a fundamentally vital role in this new system, with its emphasis on localism, and the government looked to these individuals to enhance existing services, plan new services and campaign for better services (Rochester et al, 2012, p 88). Efforts to lighten the load on public services by using volunteers continued during the recession of the 1970s and economic crises of the 1980s. With the link between volunteering and employability firmly on Margaret Thatcher's Conservative Party agenda from 1979 onwards, volunteer-based programmes, such as the Urban Programme, were introduced to combat unemployment and urban decay (Rochester et al, 2012).

Since the 1960s, the government has promoted volunteering to a greater or lesser extent through a number of programmes and policies. These were largely promoted according to a combination of party-political agendas, expediency and sometimes 'serendipity' (Rochester et al, 2012, p 84). Very often, the expediency element was driven by the soaring cost of maintaining public services and responding to the ever-increasing public demands being placed upon them.

When John Major took over as Conservative Party leader and prime minister in November 1990, he inherited an education system from Margaret Thatcher that had suffered a considerable decline in investment and a huge increase in the inequality of provision. Expenditure on education as a percentage of gross domestic product (GDP) had reached a high point of 6.5% in 1975/76 under the Labour government led by James Callaghan, but by the mid-1980s, it had dropped to 5.3% and it remained below that level under both Thatcher and Major. Capital spending on schools (mainly used for buildings and premises) by the mid-1990s was less than half of what it was in the 1970s (Jones, 2003, p 112). In terms of socio-economic deprivation and inequality, when Margaret Thatcher became prime minister in 1979, around 10% of children lived in households whose income was less than half the national average; by 1993, the figure was 33% (Oppenheim and Lister, 1997, p 24). Furthermore, a report by Ofsted in 1997 revealed that state schools with large numbers of children from poor homes were by far the worst performers when it came to General Certificate of Secondary Education (GCSE) results, and it was precisely this type of school that also struggled to recruit school governors (Sallis, 1988).

It was John Major's Conservative government that introduced the most ambitious volunteer programme that the country had ever seen when it launched the 'Make a Difference Campaign'. This was the first indication that the government was to take a more integrated approach to volunteering throughout the whole of the UK. This approach was continued by the New Labour administration in 1997 when they embarked upon a number of initiatives and programmes aimed at the voluntary sector (Kendall and Knapp, 1996); however, the funding for most of these programmes was restricted to England only.

Volunteering, 2010–15

Volunteering has always been synonymous with public sector reform, and the beginning of the period between 2010 and 2015 was marked by a speech by Prime Minister David Cameron, leader of the Coalition government, who declared his intention to reform public services, stating that he wished 'one of the great achievements of this Government to be the complete modernisation of our public services' (Cameron, 2010).

The central tenets of Cameron's ambitious reform programme built on many facets of New Labour's programme for reform: more competition between services; greater levels of marketisation and choice; and more transparency in public service standards and delivery. However, where New Labour's programme had involved high levels of public spending, the Coalition's featured a range of austerity measures designed to combat what they saw as an 'over-bloated welfare state'. Under New Labour, public spending had reached a historic high of 48% of GDP by 2009/10, 'leaving Britain with the "largest deficit in its peacetime history at 11% of the GDP"' (Parliament, 2010b).

Cameron's view of the 'Big Society' was built upon a vision that envisaged a far greater role for the voluntary and third sector in providing services that had previously been provided by the state. This was designed to take advantage of increasing competition between providers while also saving money. However, an emphasis on payment by results 'made it difficult for smaller voluntary groups with poor cash flow to compete … this tipped the scales in favour of private sector firms which won some 90% of the prime contracts, leaving the third sector as sub-contractors' (Burton, 2014, p 41). This was not part of the vision, but the vision was ambitious, as David Lewis describes in this quotation:

> The first is concerned with the promotion of volunteerism and philanthropy, with citizens being encouraged to give up more of their time for free and to set aside more resources to help others. The second is a new emphasis on localism and community-level empowerment, based on the principle that voluntary and community groups can and should play a more central role in running public services … finally the Big Society brings a new and more aggressive approach to public sector reform that seeks to cut red tape and encourage innovation.… the Big Society Idea is therefore part of government's attempt to continue the reshaping of relationships between citizens, the third sector, the state and the market. (Lewis, 2012, p 179)

Yet, despite this emphasis on volunteering and the 'Big Society' rhetoric surrounding it, in England, rates of volunteering remained fairly stable, apart from a peak in 2005, when 44% of respondents to the annual Citizenship Survey (Communities.gov.uk, 2011) reported that they had volunteered in the past year. This rate declined slowly to 39% by 2010/11. More recent statistics briefly hinted at a return to the peak-level figures (44%) in 2012/13, only to decrease again (41%) the following year and remaining similar in 2015 (Institute for Volunteering Research, 2015). The Big Society idea has since been criticised by a number of academics and writers as an anachronism based on a rosy view of society that departed substantially from the reality of austerity, recession and mass unemployment that characterised the period from 2009 to 2015. Michael Burton, in his book on the politics of public sector reform, refers to other similar idealised policies 'aiming to rebuild civil society – for example the Soviet Bloc in the period following the collapse of centralised state control, "a project that too was riddled with flaws"' (Burton, 2014, p 42).

There is no doubt that volunteering contributes an enormous amount to the economy: work by Volunteering England (2009) put the annual output figure for all formal and informal volunteers at £45.1 billion. Volunteering is also widely recognised to contribute a great deal to the well-being of individuals, to the tune of around £70 billion per year (Fujiwara et al, 2013). Their research pointed out that those unable to volunteer had a 1.9% reduction in life satisfaction (Fujiwara et al, 2013, p 1). However, the same research revealed that although around 40% of the population volunteer at least once per year, frequent volunteering is lower and has flatlined in recent years. Some research indicates that there is a minority subset of the population, a '"civic core" of people who contribute a disproportionate amount of time and money: 31 percent of the population provides 87% of voluntary hours and 79% of charitable giving' (Fujiwara et al, 2013, p 3). The Cabinet Office (2011) 'National Survey of Charities and Social Enterprises' also revealed that 'geographic distribution of the core is uneven, favouring more prosperous areas' (Fujiwara et al, 2013, p 3).

In terms of school governance, there is little doubt that school governors contribute an immense amount to the education budget. A recent report by James et al (2014, p 33) revealed that governors contribute in excess of £1 billion per year to the education budget in England; this estimation is based on time spent on governing along with employer time given to governance.

In terms of education, the sweeping changes to the structure and architecture of the system within the period 2010–15, designed to fit with the neoliberal ideals of choice and competition, combined with the steady decline in volunteer numbers across the public services, were to place unparalleled challenges on school governance and educational accountability more broadly. However, before moving on to consider these challenges and how they came to a head with the Trojan Horse affair, it is necessary to take a brief look at how the system of school governing evolved and was moulded and shaped over the periods outlined earlier.

School governing in a changing system

School governing – the governing of schools by unpaid volunteers – dates back some 600 years. It was first introduced to ensure financial probity in schools in order to reassure educational philanthropists (and the Church) that their money was being put to good use. School governing was subject to one of the first great shake-ups in its evolution when the Education Act 1944 laid down the partnership between central and local government and set out in some detail the roles and responsibilities of governors and the division of responsibilities between LEAs and individual schools. The Act changed the shape and form of governing bodies or boards, increasing their powers and specifically articulating their modus operandi.

The system of school governance remained relatively unchallenged and unchanged until the mid-1960s, when the Labour Party, which had been out of office for a considerable time, decided to implement a project that would open up school governing to far more stakeholders than ever before. The changes, first piloted in Sheffield, gave rise to the Taylor report (Parliament, 1977), which recommended that schools should have far larger and more participatory governing bodies than ever before, and that these bodies should consist of five main stakeholder representatives: the relevant LEA; parents; teachers; pupils;

and the local community. The report was also responsible for instigating training for governors, recommending that all LEAs provide at least a basic training. The Education Act 1980, which followed hard on the heels of the report, extended democratic participation by allowing any governor to stand as chair – a role that had been open only to LEA governors up until then. These changes were noteworthy in their capacity to reduce the power of LEAs, which, at the time of writing, continues to be eroded. They also marked one of the first attempts to introduce stakeholder representation into education – a move that, following the Education Reform Act 1988, would eventually lead to the interpellation of parents as consumers:

> The changes were consolidated in the 1986 Education Act which focused on productive partnership between central and local government and finally put paid to the dominance of governing bodies by LEA representatives. The Act also introduced the idea of governors reporting to parents – a move which highlighted the central role of schools within their communities – an element all but negated in the later and far reaching Education Reform Act of 1988. (Maclure, 1989)

The radical changes to education brought about by the Education Reform Act 1988 are documented in numerous publications, many of which focus on the huge impact it had. However, in order to understand why this particular Act is so important in terms of school governing today, it needs to be placed against the background of sweeping political changes and the ideas driving them.

The Education Reform Act 1988, public services and the implications for the transformation of school governing, 1988–2010

The Education Reform Act 1988 came at a time when pressures on UK public services had been building for some time and successive governments were demanding new ways of thinking about both costs and standards across the public sector. The then Conservative government's response to this was to establish the Audit Commission for local authorities in England and Wales. Set up in 1982 through the Local Government Finance Act, the Audit Commission began work as a public corporation on 1 April 1983 under the leadership of Michael Heseltine, former Conservative cabinet minister, aiming to 'rein back irresponsible spending by local government' (Campbell-Smith, 2008, p 288).

It was run by 16 executive commissioners under Heseltine and, according to Duncan Campbell-Smith (2008), possessed a number of advantages for a government that had become disillusioned with the ways in which local government spending was managed. The first advantage included the ability to work with the speed and agility of any private sector consultancy to analyse any of the public services beyond Westminster. The second, which proved equally seductive – not only to the Conservative government that created it, but also to every government up until it was dismantled in 2015 – was its ability to operate within Whitehall while remaining entirely outside of the civil service. It also had the advantage of being independent, a status that included 'a licence to publish unsolicited critiques of impact on economy, effectiveness and efficiency of the public services' (Campbell-Smith, 2008, p 2).

The Audit Commission began its critique of the education sector with a report in 1988 entitled *Surplus capacity in secondary schools* (Audit Commission, 1988). The report was a 'damning critique on the Local Education Authority's failure to adjust to the baby boom era, a failure that resulted in 24% spare capacity and wasted funding on school places' (Campbell-Smith, 2008, p 224). This was followed in the same year by a report that instructed LEAs in how to delegate management authority to individual schools. The report, entitled *Local management of schools: A note to local education* (Audit Commission, 1988a), constituted an extensive list of instructions contained in 200 paragraphs and no less than 57 steps, which is an indication of the government's lack of trust in LEAs to implement the new structures. The government had also been convinced for some time that LEAs were not providing an efficient service with regard to education (among other areas of public services). In fact, Nigel Lawson, Conservative financial secretary to the Treasury, went so far as to be open in his view that local government should be cut out of the education sector altogether (Lawson, 1992).

The Education Reform Act 1988 was designed to implement a market ideology into the education sector while also attempting to standardise it by imposing a national curriculum. While it effectively centralised education by removing power from LEAs and greatly increasing the powers of the secretary of state for education, it also placed governors in the spotlight through its emphasis on school self-management. This was achieved by the introduction of Local Management of Schools (LMS), a move that reflected the neoliberal turn adopted by many countries in an effort to find 'the right blend of state, market and democratic institutions to guarantee peace, inclusion, wellbeing and stability' (Harvey, 2005, p 10), all elements thought to be threatened by successive economic downturns in capitalist systems.

In England, the reports of the Audit Commission only served to confirm what the government had suspected for some time: that the education system, in common with other public services, was bloated and inefficient; furthermore, it was driven by the 'producer' interests of those who worked in it – teachers, head teachers and local councillors – and less by the needs of its stakeholders. Clarke and Newman (1997, p 44) refer to this as the demise of 'the bureau professional regime', a regime heavily criticised, particularly by the New Right, for its 'monopolistic features, self-interest and absence of accountability'.

Newly created autonomy, combined with the government push for efficiency in public services and the demise of the bureau-professional machine, affected school governance in two principal ways. First, by placing more responsibility on governors to hold schools to account, it resulted in a far greater impetus to engage governors from the business community: 'schools need[ed] to run like companies with the governing bodies being boards of directors and the head teachers the managing directors' (Thody, 1994, p 22). Second, it required a system of accountability that would hold both schools and governors to account, a system that would replace the current schools inspectorate (HMIs), which had been suspected of becoming too close to those under inspection for some time, with a new body. This body would be more ostensibly rigorous in its approach: it would not only hold schools to account, but would publish information on standards; and it would equip parents in the same way as any consumer of a service, with information that would allow them to make an informed choice (see Baxter and Clarke, 2013). How this was implemented and what effect it would have on governors is discussed more fully in Chapter Four.

The changes instigated by the Education Reform Act 1988 and the ideologies associated with it – consumerism, choice and the market – have continued to gain pace since then. As Deem et al (1995) pointed out in their study of school governors, these traits were not just confined to a single government or political ideology, but gained in popularity under both the New Labour administration (1997–2010) and the Conservative–Liberal Democrat Coalition government of 2010–15. The Conservative government, voted in on 7 May 2015, shows no signs of moving away from these priorities, and the education system today is more fragmented and complex than at any time in its long and chequered history.

Challenges for school governance

This leaves school governance today facing three key issues: new school structures and complex multi-level forms of governance; increased levels of responsibility and concomitant accountability; and a dearth of external support by LEAs.

In order to build on the autonomy created by the Education Reform Act 1988 and, at the same time, address the problem of falling standards – particularly in schools in areas of high socio-economic deprivation – the New Labour government under Tony Blair set up the academies project (Ball, 2009; Woods and Brighouse, 2014). Although it was a flagship policy, at first, only failing schools were permitted to become academies, but in 2010, the project was intensified and widened with the establishment of the Academies Act 2010. Under the new regulations, outstanding schools could also opt for academy status. During the Conservative–Liberal Democrat Coalition government's term in office (2010–15), the powers incorporated in the Act were used to advance the neoliberal belief in the efficiency of the market, enabling Ofsted to force failing schools to become academies (Gorard, 1999). Between 2010 and 2015, more than 900 schools judged to be weak were turned into sponsored academies – that is, taken over by schools judged to be good or outstanding – and a further 2,800 were granted academy status. By 7 May 2015, the number of academies in England had risen to 4,000, almost 20 times as many as there were in May 2010, when all 203 academies were sponsored secondary schools (Gov.uk, 2015).

However, academies were not the only type of school to increase in number during the Coalition government's five years in power. Since 2010, 250 free schools – schools set up and run by teachers, parents and charities – have opened. The free school project, championed by ex-Education Minister Michael Gove, was an integral part of the Big Society vision (DfE, 2011a). Modelled partly on the US system of charter schools and partly on the Swedish model of free schools (see Wilborg, 2010), they were intended to provide parents and community groups with the ultimate in choice – their own school, established and run by stakeholders. Since then, the project has been dogged by controversy, with high-profile school failures such as the demise of the Durham Free School, which was ordered to close because of its failure to improve after being placed in special measures – the lowest grade awarded by the schools' inspectorate, Ofsted (Adams, 2015).

In addition to the autonomy offered by free school and academy status, English education has experienced a rise in the number of schools grouping together under a single governing body. A body of research, particularly over the last 10 years, has pointed to a number of benefits of collaboration between schools. These include: the sharing of professional knowledge; continuity between phases (infant through middle and secondary); the homogenisation of school budgets to provide more efficient budgeting; the sharing of key staff in order to widen the curriculum; the sharing of resources and services, such as human resources, financial services and other support services; and the sharing of head teachers at a time when it is becoming increasingly difficult to recruit them (see, eg, Higham and Hopkins, 2007; Lindsay et al, 2007; Chapman et al, 2009).

These new structures have had profound implications for governing bodies, not only in terms of the number of schools under their tenure, but also in terms of the multi-level systems of governance that have emerged because of these new structures. In some cases, governors may be responsible for a number of schools, supported by local governing groups that have consultative but no decision-making powers, and this has raised questions over what it really means to be a school governor (see, eg, Chapman et al, 2010; Baxter and Wise, 2013).

The second major challenge for school governance arises from the increased regulatory emphasis placed upon it by the English schools inspectorate, Ofsted. The plethora of autonomous schools free from local authority control has left the government with a serious accountability deficit. In its haste to implement the academy and free schools project, the Coalition government paid little heed to the erosion of the existing accountability system managed by LEAs and Ofsted. The autonomy possessed by academies and free schools left them directly accountable to the Education Secretary – a position that was clearly unsustainable given the rapid rise in numbers mentioned earlier. Despite valiant efforts to rise to the challenges of the new system, Ofsted, the schools watchdog set up in 1992 under John Major's Conservative government, struggled, not only with new structures, but equally with the constant pressure to improve standards, a pressure rendered all the more pressing by newspaper headlines comparing results from international programmes such as PISA and proclaiming England's standards to be slipping.

The third major challenge arises from the steady erosion of the powers of LEAs. As mentioned earlier in this chapter, successive governments have become increasingly disillusioned with the performance of local government. The rise of the Audit Commission, the inception of LMS in the Education Reform Act 1988 and the establishment of Ofsted in 1992 as part of John Major's Citizen's Charter all combined to undermine LEAs (for a full account of the demise of LEAs, see Sharp, 2002; for further discussion, see also Chapter Four).

From 2010, the pressure increased. Alongside structural changes in the national system of education have come new and evolving conceptions of what constitutes 'a good education'. As mentioned earlier, these conceptions have arisen, in part, due to the substantial influence of PISA. This particular comparator has, since its inception in 2000, developed as a major influence on education, with an almost hegemonic capacity to influence politicians and the media. In 2012, 510,000 students in 65 economies took part in its assessment of reading, maths and science, representing a staggering 28 million 15 year olds globally (OECD, 2015). PISA is far more than an international league table, in the political world and as a policy influencer and shaper, it has achieved an influence paralleled only by organisations such as the World Bank. It has become the driver for inspection systems throughout Europe (and beyond), systems employed by government to raise standards in education (see, eg, Grek and Lindgren, 2014). It also exerts an enormous influence on the media, both through its own press department and through the attention it receives from the national press in member states. Unfortunately, England has not fared particularly well in the tables, provoking outcry around 'falling standards' and the lack of social mobility (for more details, see Chapter Four). The Coalition government, intent on raising standards, mandated that Ofsted not only examine the performance of schools, but also turn its attention to LEAs. A series of high-profile reports by the inspectorate were used alongside comprehensive data visualisations (Ofsted, 2013b) to support the view that the academy and free school projects were fully justified given the level of failure among LEAs (Paton, 2012). This, combined with sweeping cuts to LEA budgets, meant that services to schools and support to governors were severely curtailed.

Ofsted responded to the challenges laid down by government with the introduction of a new inspection regime in 2012. Within it, governors are placed as central to the leadership and management of a school (or group of schools). They are judged on their capacity to strategically lead the school (Ofsted, 2012) and their ability to 'challenge and support the school and senior leadership team so that weaknesses are tackled decisively and statutory responsibilities met'

(Ofsted, 2012, p 14). The integration of governors' work under a single judgement of leadership and management rather than rendering it separately, as in previous iterations of the framework, has had profound implications for the regulation of the governor role and how it is regulated (see, eg, Ofsted, 1993, 2009).

These pressures have combined to create what James et al (2011) termed 'the perfect storm': on the one hand, increased regulatory pressures, new governance structures and responsibilities; while, on the other, lack of support and coherent local oversight, creating multiple demands on governors. The Trojan Horse affair revealed just how much of a toxic combination this would prove to be.

TWO

THE TROJAN HORSE AFFAIR: MEDIA PHENOMENON AND POLICY DRIVER

Introduction: a media frenzy

The Trojan Horse affair made headline news on 2 March 2014 with an article by Richard Karaj and Sian Griffiths, writing in *The Sunday Times* newspaper. Karaj, an established journalist within the Murdoch Group, known for his extensive writing on Islamic matters, had a reputation for provocative writing and the use of polarising emotive language (Griffiths et al, 2013).

The article, with the title 'Islamist plot to take over schools' (Kerbaj and Griffiths, 2014), ran with the leader 'Leaked paper reveals an alleged plan to target ailing schools, force out heads and convert classes to Islamic principles', and reported details of an apparent plot by Muslim fundamentalists to destabilise and take over state schools in England. In order to appreciate why this article was so powerful, and why it became so influential, it is outlined in full in Box 2.1.

Box 2.1: Article as it appeared in *The Sunday Times*, 2 March 2014

AN APPARENT plot by Muslim fundamentalists to destabilise and take over state schools in England is being investigated by council officials and monitored by police.

Birmingham city council began an inquiry after the circulation of what purport to be strategy documents outlining ways of ousting head teachers in Muslim areas of the city in order to establish schools run on Islamic principles.

The anonymous documents were passed by the council to West Midlands police. The paperwork, which appears to have been written by disaffected Muslims, has been leaked to *The Sunday Times*. It is not known whether the council's investigation which was opened in November, has established the authorship of the documents.

The revelation comes as a further setback for the government's academies and free schools programme, where institutions are freed from council control and run as semi-independent bodies by a sponsor or trust.

The documents highlight a five-step strategy, allegedly written by unnamed Salafists – fundamentalist Muslims – to remove unwanted head teachers. The schools targeted include failing institutions that could be turned into academies.

The Sunday Times revealed last week that Park View Academy in Birmingham is being investigated by the Department for Education for allegedly side-lining non-Muslim staff and trying to teach Islamic studies, despite not being a faith-based state school.

The documents suggest that the strategy, called Operation Trojan Horse, should be used in Bradford and Manchester as well as Birmingham. 'We have an obligation to our children to fulfil our roles and ensure these schools are run on Islamic principles,' they argue.

The papers say this first step is to identify poor-performing state schools in Muslim areas; then Salafist parents in each school are encouraged to complain that teachers are 'corrupting children with sex education, teaching about homosexuals, making their children say Christian prayers and mixed swimming and sports.'

The next steps are to 'parachute in' Muslim governors 'to drip-feed our ideal for a Muslim school' and stir up staff to urge the council to investigate. The strategy stresses the importance of having an 'English face among the staff group to make it more believable'.

Finally anonymous letters are to be circulated to MPs, press and ministers. 'All these things will work towards wearing the head down, removing their resolve and weakening their mind set so they eventually give up.'

Birmingham schools named as targets in the document include Regents Park, where the head teacher, Tina Ireland, was given an 'outstanding' Office for Standards in Education, Children's Services and Skills (Ofsted) report but resigned last year amid questions over the school's exam results. Others are Adderley Primary School and Saltley School, a specialist science college where the head, Balwant Bains, resigned last year. Bains quit after an Ofsted report concluded that he had a 'dysfunctional' relationship with governors.

Ahson Mohammed, the interim head teacher at Saltley, was appointed in November after Bain's resignation.

Mohammed said the school categorically denied any suggestion that Bains resigned as a result of pressure from Muslim extremists.

'The leadership team of the school has been appointed by the ... same governing body which has been here for a long time,' he said. 'The previous head teacher was also non-Muslim. Balwant Bains was also non-Muslim.

'So in reality whether they were Muslim or non-Muslim is obviously not the issue. What they want is quality leadership, not what faith or what race you are from.'

Mohammed said the school has been closely monitored since Bains' departure. 'We have been under extensive scrutiny, both by Ofsted [and] by the local authority.... Where we are not is the school is stabilised, the school is functioning and has been named as being one of the top 100 [most improved] schools in the UK.

Source: Kerbaj and Griffiths (2014).

The article, appearing in the 'News' section of *The Sunday Times*, was powerful and influential for a number of reasons. The language was particularly provocative, using terms normally associated with counterterrorism activities. Words such as 'plot', 'strategy', 'targets', 'targeted', 'operation', 'wearing down', 'weakening their mind set', 'closely monitored', 'parachute in' and 'extremist' tapped into public fears around extremism that had been building in the media for some time. One particularly toxic aspect of the article was the conflation of the term Muslim with the more sinister cult of Islamism, reinforcing Islamophobia, or mistrust of all things pertaining to Islam, and echoing numerous articles, books and negative media coverage that had been emerging for some time, particularly since the 9/11 terrorist attacks (see Abbas, 2005; Morey and Yaquin, 2011; Petley, 2013).

The article was also powerful in making a textual link with the earlier debate around Ofsted's criticism of the Al-Madinah school in Derby, a school declared inadequate in every area and closed down while allegations were investigated. Unusually, the report on the Al-Madinah school was published in full in *The Guardian* – a move that gave it far greater public prominence than would usually be accorded to a failing school. The leader used a political hook to engage readers – a strategy that became increasingly prevalent in articles that appeared throughout 2013 and 2014: 'Controversial free school at the heart of row between Labour and Tories over Michael Gove's reform programme condemned as "dysfunctional"' (Ofsted, 2013c).

The media also highlighted the religious elements of the findings, as the following quotation illustrates:

> Unnamed female members of staff also said they had been forced to conform to a strict dress code including wearing a head scarf or hijab – regardless of whether they were Muslims. However, the interim head teacher said he had not received any complaints about the dress code and denied boys and girls were segregated in class. (Garner, 2013)

These earlier articles had helped to sensitise the media to any reference making mention of Muslims, and many reporters immediately made a link between the alleged plot, the government, purported Islamist agendas and extremism.

The link between the Trojan Horse affair and an Islamist agenda was also undoubtedly enhanced by a textual link between that and use of the term 'Trojan Horse', which had appeared much earlier in a book first published in 2006 and written by then Education Secretary Michael Gove. The book was a strongly worded account of how a lack of "'[m]oral clarity" in British State Policy over the last 15 years [had] been responsible for the rise of Islamism' (Gove, 2006). On page 84, the first lines of a chapter entitled 'The Trojan Horse' point out what Gove perceives to be fundamental flaws in this policy:

> First has been the willingness to extend a 'covenant of security' to known Islamist activists within the UK … the second, the determined playing down of the Islamist terror threat … the British State persisted for years in believing that those who posed a direct danger to the country were a tiny renegade minority with no important connection to a broader ideological network … third has been the failure to scrutinize, monitor or check the actions, funding and operation of those committed to spreading the Islamist word within Britain. (Gove, 2006, p 84)

The link between the 'Trojan Horse' and Gove's earlier imaginings was hard to ignore – particularly with regard to its 'story value' in enhancing the 'plot' within a rapidly developing crisis (Vogler, 2007), and certain news outlets embraced its power as a link between the Education Secretary's earlier concerns and the so-called 'plot' as it unfolded.

The techniques used in this and subsequent articles on the Trojan Horse affair are not dissimilar to those used to provoke other moral panics, such as Bob Franklin's account of how a 'vituperative media' created opprobrium around poverty and those claiming welfare benefits in order to pave the way for welfare reform (Franklin, 2002, p 11) (explored in more detail in Chapter Three). In this and other similar cases, a crisis was created and then manipulated in order to produce a 'defining' event, crafted by the government and media in such a way as to exemplify major failings in policy and, as a consequence, prove to be a driver for 'reform' in a particular policy area.

Even though many suspected at the time that the whole affair was a hoax – as Robin Richardson points out, the article title was written in inverted commas to signal doubt – the political fallout was wide-ranging and spectacular. A search on the news database Lexis Nexus from the period 3 March 2014 to 3 March 2015 with the search terms 'Trojan Horse + schools + Birmingham' revealed over 3,000 articles, and this does not include all of the blogs, personal websites and other social media feeds that also produced commentary on the affair. Of these articles, 1,787 featured in national newspapers. Combining the three search terms 'Trojan Horse + schools + governors' revealed a total of 1,775 articles overall, with 879 featuring in national newspapers. Of these articles, some 737 also contained the term 'Islam' and 387 the term 'Islamist'. One of the most provocative headlines appeared in the *Birmingham Mail* on 7 March 2014: 'Jihadist plot to take over schools'.

The Arabic word 'Jihad' is often translated as 'holy war', but according to the dictionary, it means 'struggling or striving'. In a religious sense, as described by the Quran and teachings, 'jihad' has a number of meanings. It can refer to internal and external efforts to be a good Muslim, as well as indicating the notion of working to inform people about the faith of Islam, and protecting the faith of Islam (Hossein et al, 2015). However, since 9/11, the word has come to be associated with terror plots, particularly in the media, where its more peaceful connotation has largely been lost.

Such was the confusion and speculation around the affair, compounded by more leaked documents, press releases by the schools involved and commentary from chairs of governors, teachers, head teachers, MPs and other community representatives, that on 22 July 2014, the BBC released a timeline to show the order of events as they unfolded (see Table 2.1). In Table 2.1, the language underlined shows how the events became increasingly conflated with terrorist activity by the use of certain 'trigger words' forming textual links to other articles on extremism. The table also gives an example of how Sir Michael Wilshaw – an individual to whom the press had already become 'sensitised' due to earlier conflict between him and then Education Secretary Michael Gove – became an eponym for Ofsted in many of the stories. It is also interesting to note that somewhere between March 2014 and when this report was produced, in many

Table 2.1: Timeline of events

Date	Event
7 March	Birmingham City Council states it is investigating a number of schools in the city after receiving a copy of an anonymous letter referring to Operation Trojan Horse – **a plot** by some Muslim groups to install governors at schools, it **claims responsibility** for ousting head teachers.
17 March	Ofsted turns up at Park View academy for a snap inspection. Two years earlier the previous school on the site had been graded outstanding. **'All schools should be like this,' Ofsted Chief Sir Michael Wilshaw had said in March 2012.**
31 March	The DfE says it is looking into claims the Trojan Horse **plot targeted** 12 schools.
9 April	Governors of Park View Educational Trust describe the ongoing investigations as a 'witch-hunt'.
14 April	Birmingham City Council says it is looking into allegations involving 25 schools in the city, including primaries, secondaries and academies. Council Leader Sir Albert Bore says he does not believe there is a 'Plot'.
15 April	West Midlands Police condemn the DfE's decision to appoint a **former national head of counter terrorism** to carry out its investigation for the message it sends.
20 April	Sir Michael Wilshaw takes personal charge of Ofsted's Trojan Horse investigations.
3 May	Sir Michael says Ofsted has inspected 21 schools in Birmingham.
3 June	Three of the schools under investigation **publish their Ofsted reports.** Nine Stiles and Small Heath are rated as 'outstanding' and Washwood Heath as 'good'.
4 June	Home Secretary Theresa May accuses Education Secretary Michael Gove of **failing to deal with an alleged Islamist plot to take over schools**. In a letter she asks whether it is true that the DfE was warned about the allegations in 2010 and Birmingham Council as far back as 2008.
9 June	Ofsted places five schools in special measures and confirms that a sixth (which was already in special measures) is 'inadequate. **Sir Michael says there is evidence of an 'organised campaign to target certain schools' and finds that some governors attempted to 'impose and promote a narrow faith-based ideology' in secular schools.** The schools involved deny any wrongdoing.

SCHOOL GOVERNANCE

Date	Event
10 June	Two academies – Park View and Nansen Primary – **are told they will lose funding,** while Oldknow Academy and Golden Hillock School are warned they too could lose funding unless concerns are addressed.
10 June	Ofsted head Sir Michael says the experience in Birmingham **could lead to snap inspections** at schools across the country.
15 June	**Vice-principal Lee Donaghy, however, said governors had been behind many of the changes that saw the school rated as outstanding by Ofsted in 2012.**
16 June	The Park View Educational Trust, which runs three of the schools put in special measures, accuses the government of 'deliberately misrepresenting' schools and describes inspections as 'woefully shoddy' and 'fatally flawed'.
4 July	Governors at Golden Hillock School said they were **not given enough time to make improvements** before a visit by Ofsted.
15 July	The board of Trustees at Park View Education Trust resign. Its chairman Tahir Alam said the decision had been made in the interests of the children. He said a **'co-ordinated and vicious' attack** by former Education Secretary Michael Gove and the Department for Education had left the three-member board with no choice but to step down. Waverley School head teacher Kamal Hanif, Greet Primary head teacher Pat Smart and King Edwards VI Five Ways head teacher Yvonne Wilkinson agree to serve on the new trust. The DfE said their appointment would allow the trust to 'address the areas for improvement raised by the Education Funding Agency and Ofsted reports and move it towards a successful sponsor'.
17 July	A leaked copy of Peter Clarke's report for the DfE finds evidence there was 'coordinated, deliberate and sustained action to introduce an intolerant and aggressive Islamist ethos into some schools in the city.' If left unchecked it would 'confine schoolchildren within an intolerant, inward looking monoculture that would severely inhibit their participation in the life of modern Britain.' Details of the report by the **former counter-terrorism chief** were leaked to *The Guardian* newspaper.

Date	Event
18 July	Birmingham City Council releases key findings from its inquiry into 25 schools. Written by Ian Kershaw, it finds **no evidence of violent extremism, radicalisation or an anti-British agenda being promoted**. However, it does warn of **governance problems in some schools**. Mr Kershaw also criticises the council's role in supporting the schools involved.
22 July	Birmingham MP, Khalid Mahmood, says teachers forced out of schools involved in the Trojan Horse allegations deserve to be compensated. He claimed at least 12 senior school staff had been bullied or forced out of their posts.
22 July	Peter Clarke's report for the DfE is officially released. Mr Clarke said his inquiry found **no evidence of extremism** but 'there are a number of people in a position of influence who either **espouse**, or **sympathise with or fail to challenge extremist views**'.

Source: BBC (2014).

articles, the Trojan Horse 'plot' lost the inverted commas signifying doubt, as Table 2.1 illustrates.

Following the affair, Ofsted and the Education Funding Agency (the body that manages £54 billion funding to support all state-provided education) finally released reports into the 21 schools that were investigated following the initial allegations. Out of the schools investigated, five were placed in special measures – the lowest Ofsted grade – with a further nine schools downgraded to 'requires improvement'. The reports were greeted with outrage by many living in the communities served by those schools – communities with high levels of ethnic minority concentration and socio-economic deprivation (Baxter, 2014b).

The media frenzy that followed the release of the reports was unprecedented. Ofsted was accused of political partiality, and in the cabinet, a high-profile row erupted between Home Secretary Theresa May and then Education Secretary Michael Gove, following the leak of a pointed letter in which May declared that concerns had been raised about the inability of local and central government to tackle allegations of similar activities raised as early as 2008 (see Table 2.1) (Adams, 2014). A Department for Education (DfE) spokesperson, speaking in *The Times*, stated that:

> The Extremists have set out over time to take over and subvert governing bodies of schools using entries in the same way as political parties have been taken over, such as Militant Tendency. Some have been very wary of drawing attention to this as it might be seen as Islamophobic. That is why there has been a reluctance to acknowledge what has been going on. (Watt and Adams, 2014)

After months of speculation and considerable unrest in the communities affected by the affair, two reports were commissioned. The first, by Ian Kershaw as Independent Chief Adviser, was for Birmingham City Council (Kershaw, 2014), and the second, by Peter Clarke, was for the DfE (Clarke, 2014). The appointment of Clarke again signified the 'unequivocal link' between the happenings at the schools in question and extremist activity. Peter Clarke, a former police commander who headed up Scotland Yard's anti-terrorism branch from 2002 until 2008, had been known as 'the face' of anti-terrorism activity since the July 2005 London bombings. A prominent media spokesman on counterterrorism activities, his appointment could not have been more inflammatory. As Chris Simms, Chief of the West Midlands Police, pointed out: 'Peter Clarke has many qualities but people will inevitably draw unwarranted conclusions from his former role as National Co-ordinator for Counter Terrorism' (BBC, 2014).

Although the Clarke report concluded that there was a 'plot', the findings of the Kershaw report contained no evidence of there ever having been one. What both reports did have in common, however, was their focus on the failings of governance in all of the schools concerned, failings that, in the opinion of both experts, had contributed in no small measure to the attempts to impose a narrow view of Islam on the curriculum of all of the schools concerned.

Kershaw outlined these failures of governance in very specific terms, stating that:

> [These] activist governors have regarded the role of being a governor as a means to an end. Where they judge a school to be failing the students, they have seen their role as one of leading change through the replacement of school leadership and an improper manipulation of school governance. There is a need to guard against this behaviour, which does not comply with local authority and school governance legal obligations. (Kershaw, 2014, p 4)

He went on to describe how:

> Due to certain weaknesses in the systems and processes that surround school governance, as well as local authority failings, this has been allowed to happen unchecked. Birmingham City Council was aware of some of these concerns, and failed to spot others when it should have done, due to a failure to join up the intelligence it did receive in relation to these schools. (Kershaw, 2014, p 5)

The Kershaw report indicated that cuts imposed on Birmingham City Council over the course of the past five years had seriously impacted on school support and overview, with staff numbers in this area being reduced from 170 to just 20.

This failing was highlighted not only in both the Kershaw and the Clarke reports, but also in a more recent report 'Extremism in schools: the Trojan Horse affair' produced by the House of Commons Education Committee (Gov.uk, 2015). This comprehensive report, which includes the formal minutes relating to the report, found failings in a number of areas. The combination of these problems had, in the view of the committee, led to the debacle and was judged to be serious, although there appeared to be little proof of an extremist plot. The committee concluded that a number of factors were responsible for the affair and that it was these, working in combination with one another, that had created the situation in Birmingham. The main factors in terms of why the affair had taken such a hold were detailed as:

- Our recent report on academies and free schools addresses many of the issues of oversight which have arisen in the context of the Trojan Horse inquiries. The greater autonomy of academies makes it easier for a group of similar-minded people to control a school. While it should be remembered that several of the governors criticised in Birmingham were local government appointees, the DfE needs to be alert to the risks of abuse of academy freedoms of all kinds and be able to respond quickly. (Paragraph 60)
- The sheer number of organisations which became involved indicated the complexity of emerging oversight arrangements for schools. The number of overlapping inquiries contributed to the sense of crisis and confusion, and the number of reports, coming out at different times and often leaked in advance, was far from helpful. (Paragraph 27)
- Ofsted's inability to identify problems at some Birmingham schools on first inspection when they were found shortly afterwards to be failing raises questions about the appropriateness of the framework and the reliability and robustness of Ofsted's judgements and how they are reached. Either Ofsted relied too heavily on raw data and did not dig deep enough on previous occasions or alternatively the schools deteriorated so quickly that Ofsted reports were rapidly out of date, or it could be that inspectors lost objectivity and came to some overly negative conclusions because of the surrounding political and media storm. Whichever of these options is closest to the truth, confidence in Ofsted has been undermined and efforts should be made by the inspectorate to restore it in Birmingham and beyond. (Paragraph 41)
- There was a proven "lack of inquisitiveness" within the Department for Education prior to the receipt of the Trojan Horse letter. Whilst this may be partially explained by the general level of awareness of such issues at the time, the timeline supplied by the DfE indicates

that the Department was slow to take an active interest between the receipt of the letter in December 2013 and March 2014 when the issue became public. This is more surprising, given the change in context and the heightened emphasis on combating radicalisation and extremism. We are not convinced that "open source checking" was a sufficient response to the seriousness of the allegations being made to the DfE. (Paragraph 26)

In terms of extremism, the report noted that 'the one example given by Ian Kershaw was clearly unacceptable and action should have been taken by the school to prevent it', but that 'a single instance does not warrant headline claims that students in Birmingham – or elsewhere in England – are being exposed to extremism by their teachers' (Parliament, 2014, p 7). The Committee also stated that it agreed with 'the Birmingham City Council Trojan Horse Review Group's assertion that it did not "Support the lazy conflation – frequently characterised in the national media in recent months – of what Ofsted have termed issues around a narrow faith based ideology and questions of radicalisation, extremism or terrorism'" (Parliament, 2014, p 7).

An independent inspectorate

Running almost in parallel to the discourse around failing schools and falling standards, a growing number of people had for some time been questioning just how impartial Ofsted really was. Sir Michael Wilshaw came to the role early in 2012 and was fêted by government for his work in turning round a failing school in an area of high deprivation (Wilshaw, 2011). In many ways, he embodied the kind of reforming zeal that the government wanted to see in all heads, particularly those in charge of poor or mediocre schools: an individual who had achieved what he had achieved 'against all odds'. In a passionate speech to the Ark Academies group in November 2011, just before taking up office as Her Majesty's Chief Inspector (HMCI), he expressed his dissatisfaction with the school system and made his feelings on accountability very plain, as this excerpt shows:

The industrial action of the mid-Eighties compounded the tensions I've already described, as did an over-cosy relationship between local authorities and teacher associations. The power of head teachers to shape and influence schools and school policy took a battering. Many distinguished heads I got to know in the early years of headship, took early retirement – bitter at the undermining of their authority, the politicisation of schools and, quite simply, worn out by industrial action. I still bear the scars of those days, not just because of poor industrial relations but also, in the context of the time, it took a very brave head, or a foolhardy one, to focus on school improvement and the issue of staff competence. (Wilshaw, 2011)

It is somewhat ironic that an individual who declared himself against the politicisation of schools should end up caught in the middle of what would become one of the biggest political scandals to hit education since the Tyndale affair some 40 years earlier (see Davis, 2002).

Ofsted was originally set up to be independent from government, as part of John Major's vision of a more responsive and public-centric public service (see Chapter Five). One of a number of quasi-autonomous non-governmental organisations (quangos) implemented under the Major administration, it was one of the few to escape the government cull of similar organisations in 2010. The mantra 'we inspect without fear or favour' features in much of its literature and is designed to make plain its independence from both government and the teaching profession. This proximity to the teaching profession, or 'inspector capture' as it is termed across the public sector, was a key driver in government dissatisfaction with the previous regime of Her Majesty's Inspectors (HMIs), operational up to 1992 (see Baxter and Clarke, 2012; Ozga et al, 2013; see also Chapter Five).

Under Sir Michael Wilshaw, Ofsted was determined to counter accusations that the organisation had a 'tickbox' mentality: that it was an organisation whose staff were often too far removed from the system that they were charged to inspect. This resulted in a remodelling of the workforce to include more head teachers as inspectors, along with a framework that reduced the number of judgements from 29 to a mere four, placing a far greater emphasis on the inspector's professional judgement (Baxter, 2013). Paradoxically, this had the effect of making the process of inspection a little less transparent than it had been, a not uncommon effect described by Clarke (2008) as a 'public service performance paradox'. This describes the seemingly paradoxical nature of attempts to remedy policy implementation problems, which only result in a range of 'different problems' (see also Baxter, 2014a).

Although the inspectorate was keen to promote its independence, media coverage of inspection between 2012 and early 2014 was riddled with references to its supposed 'cosiness' with government. It appeared to many that far from being the 'independent body' it purported to be, Ofsted was portrayed instead as a mere 'tool' of government, complicit in carrying out Michael Gove's 'ideological agenda' to convert failing schools into academies (Gunter, 2011), despite evidence from a number of reports, including one by the House of Commons Education Committee (HCEC, 2014–15), suggesting that becoming an academy is far from guaranteed to raise standards.

In January 2014, a row broke out between the Education Secretary and HMCI, as Howard Stevenson, professor of education at the University of Nottingham, reported in his blog:

> It is not very often that an education story is the lead item on the BBC's Today Programme, but the apparent sacking of Baroness Morgan, the Chair of Ofsted, was one such occasion. It followed hard on the heels of news that Sir Michael Wilshaw was 'spitting blood' that elements associated with the Conservative Party, some with close links to Michael Gove, were briefing against the Chief Inspector. Both Labour and Liberal Democrats argued that Michael Gove was acting 'politically' and that Ofsted's 'independence' was being compromised. (Stevenson, 2014)

Former Education Secretary Estelle Morris, writing in *The Guardian* in February 2014, argued that the reason for the fallout was that HMCI was *too* independent, finding faults with academies and free schools and thereby 'undermining' Gove's ideological project to convert schools – an ideology that also appeared to support didactic forms of teaching (the teacher standing at the front dispensing 'knowledge'). This ideology that has for some time now been associated through the media with Conservative thinking on education, as former Education Secretary Estelle Morris explained in a recent interview:

> "People have historically associated different political parties with particular education policies: the political Right have often been thought to be strong on promoting the teaching of good basic skills and strong discipline and the political Left have often been associated, for example, with a broader curriculum and children being more active in learning. This is a bit of a parody but you still get that interpretation in some of the press." (Estelle Morris, interview, October 2015)

Although there was some attempt to palliate the situation, with statements from Michael Gove in the press appearing to negate the accusations, the damage had been done – particularly to the inspectorate, which was brought into further disrepute by a number of highly critical articles, such as the one written by Dr David Green, Director of Civitas (The Institute for the Study of Civil Society). Writing in *The Spectator*, Green criticised the inspectorate and directly attacked HMCI for what he described as Ofsted's deliberate undermining of the whole of the free school and academies project: 'Free schools and academies were introduced to encourage innovation, and it is Civitas' contention that this independence is being undermined by Ofsted' (Green, 2014).

These intense political debates brought education right to the forefront of reporting – not a position to which it had been formerly accustomed (see Chapter Two). With the media fully sensitised to the three main strands of debate – Ofsted's independence, the clash between HMCI and Education Secretary Michael Gove and growing public concern about school autonomy – the stage was set for one of the most intense education media moments of the 21st century, one that placed governors firmly in the spotlight.

The final outcome? Aftermath

The extent to which the affair could be said to be a 'media sensation' was reflected in its wide international reach, making not only national, but international, news. International reporting on the affair placed it firmly in the realm of extremism, as illustrated by this example from *M Europe*, an offshoot of the French newspaper *Le Monde*:

> L'infiltration par les extrémismes musulmans de six écoles publiques de la cité des Midlands relance, non seulement, le débat sur l'évolution de la société multiculturelle britannique mais encore, divise le gouvernement de coalition conservateur-libéral-démocrate du premier ministre, David Cameron. [The infiltration by the Moslem extremists into six public schools in the Midlands once again not only kindles the debate on the evolution of British multicultural society, but more importantly divides Prime Minister David Cameron's coalition government.] (Roche, 2014)

The issue clearly touched a nerve with many other countries also struggling with integration issues, and, as in the preceding translation, the language often lost any sense of nuance, a factor that only served to further conflate Muslims with Islamism. This provoked a chain reaction, increasing levels of Islamophobia at an international level (see, eg, Sinclair, 2012, 2013).

Despite the outcomes of three major reports, none of which uncovered evidence of extremist activity, the affair had a profound effect on policy and inspection practices. It had also revealed that the rapid growth of the market-based school system was riddled with major structural defects in the areas of both the support and accountability of schools. What is more, it was becoming increasingly clear that these issues would not be remedied overnight – there would be no 'quick fix'.

Another no less important and distressing effect of the affair and the way in which it was reported by the media and handled by the government was its profound effect on school communities, not just in Birmingham, but more widely (see, eg, Bassey, 2014). The use of inflammatory language and the conflation of issues of school governance with specious 'terrorist' activities created tension and, in some cases, animosity within communities; the implications of this are discussed more fully in Chapters Three and Seven.

The Trojan Horse affair was wide-ranging in its influence of public opinion and created a discourse, a 'specific ensemble of ideas, concepts and categorizations that are produced, reproduced and transformed to give meaning to physical and social relations' (Hajer, 1995, p 44). It raised public awareness of radicalisation in a way that, despite the government's best efforts, the Prevent Strategy had failed to do. It also created certain 'norms' that went towards developing public conceptualisations of what schools should be doing in order to counter extremism in all its forms (Hajer, 1993). These were then employed to justify the whole raft of measures designed to prevent any transgressions of this nature in the future. The understandings that were communicated via this 'discourse' were particularly valuable in justifying wide-ranging changes to inspection policy, changes that gave the inspectorate an opportunity to redeem itself in the eyes of the public. These changes in terms of school governor accountability are discussed in Chapter Five and the affair's impact on policy is discussed in Chapter Seven.

The affair also illustrated the power of the media and the ways in which a narrative was created and crafted, linking poor governance with radicalisation and extremism, and Muslims with Islamism. The ways in which these links were crafted and effected are outlined in Chapter Three.

THREE

SCHOOL GOVERNORS
IN THE MEDIA

Introduction

The Trojan Horse affair did not occur in isolation, but in common with many such 'defining episodes' manifested in the guise of a culmination of a number of factors: contextual, cultural and political. As Chapter Two reported, one of the defining factors surrounding the event was the way in which it was crafted by the media and manipulated by both the media and the government to such an extent that it became impossible to understand whether this was an education scandal or a terrorist threat. In order to examine the event in more detail and to examine why it was so influential in terms of later policymaking (see Chapter Seven), this chapter places the affair within the context of what is known as the 'mediatisation of education policy' – a field of research that explores and examines the complex ways in which the media influences and shapes policy.

In this chapter, I explore some aspects that have emerged from research into the complex relationship between education policy and the media, whilst Chapter Four draws on national news reports and research from a media analysis to explore the changing portrayal of school governors in the media within the period 2009–15. In order to understand how media articulations are influenced by journalists and editors, the chapter also draws on interviews with media professionals in order to explore journalists' perceptions of what makes for a good story in education and how the media becomes 'sensitised' to stories in a particular area. In the final section, I turn to the period directly leading up to the Trojan Horse affair in 2014, examining how the 'scene was set' for one of the high-profile educational scandals of the decade.

As described in Chapter One, when the Coalition government came to office in 2010, its aim was to expand the voluntary sector as part of its Big Society project (Rochester et al, 2012). In its drive to do so, it placed considerable emphasis on voluntarism and democratic participation in the running of the public sector. Unfortunately, this went hand in hand with both a global and a national recession, financially impacting on public services, local government and third sector organisations – traditionally, the three largest employers of volunteer staff. Since then, reductions in funding have impacted adversely on organisations' capacity to recruit volunteers (through lack of funds for publicity), and have led to reductions in levels of volunteer support and training – two areas that are vital in the formation and sustenance of resilient working identities (Harrison, 1995; Cordingley et al, 2005; Henderson, 2011). As described earlier, there have been a number of studies into the influence of culture and context upon certain groups within society, and writers such as Anthony Giddens (1991) and Stuart Hall (1996, 1997) have been highly influential in linking personal and working identities by the ways in which individuals are 'positioned' in society (Giddens, 1984, p 84). Some of the most in-depth work into volunteer identities and the ways in which they are influenced by culture has been carried out by writers working in the Far East. Lynne Nakano (2000, p 93), writing about Japanese volunteer identities, indicated the very powerful way that volunteer identities (*borantia* in Japanese) have emerged as 'an alternative and supplement to mainstream life paths' and how this was enhanced by the many and varied media describing the ways in which volunteers contribute to society, as she recounts here:

Libraries and bookstores are stocked with handbooks offering advice and encouragement to would-be volunteers, national newspapers regularly feature articles on individuals who volunteer at grassroots and international levels, and employers (including the government) offer 'borantia leave.' During which employees may volunteer on company time. (Nakano, 2000, p 94)

In her article, she describes how the term '*borantia*' is used 'to refer to an individual who on his or her own initiative helps others in a spirit of goodwill' (Nakano, 2000, p 25). She continues: '[a word that was] virtually unknown twenty years ago, borantia has become a socially recognised identity and an accepted part of national policy, popular consciousness, and everyday vocabulary' (Nakano, 2000, p 93). The Japanese media has played a substantial part in making volunteering a symbol of social transformation, a phenomenon that emerged from several events in which volunteers played prominent roles, most notably, the 1995 Hanshin-Awaji earthquake and a 1997 oil spill from a sinking Russian tanker off the Japan coast. Pointing out that 'As the values of the period of economic growth were questioned, the mass media became increasingly responsive to alternative values and lifestyles' (Nakano, 2000, p 94), she asserts that it was largely the portrayal in the media of volunteering as a valid and authentic occupation that influenced the sheer speed at which it became embedded in Japanese culture, in essence, becoming 'an acceptable form of establishing oneself as a productive member of society' (Nakano, 2000, p 95).

Nakano's work, along with that of others in the field, argues that these volunteer identities must necessarily be imagined in the culture of the society in which they are based (Nakano, 2000, p 95; Slay and Smith, 2011) and must be considered alongside the prevailing political environment and ideological stance of the current administration (Hall, 1995). In order to understand the important part that the media plays in education policy, the next part of the chapter investigates the phenomenon of 'mediatisation', a term that describes the ways in which the media forms and shapes policy formation and implementation.

The mediatisation of policy

The influence of the media on policy creation and implementation has been recognised for some time now and has been the focus of research both within and outside the field of education (see, eg, Wallace, 1997; Rawolle, 2007; Strömbäck, 2008; Reunanen et al, 2010; Van Aelst et al, 2013). The term 'mediatisation' describes the 'process by which everyday practices and social relations are historically shaped by mediating technologies and media organisations' (Lundby, 2009, p 33), and although the term suggests that it describes the relationship between media organisations and their publics, it is far broader than that, 'encompassing the relationship between all societal institutions: government; church; commerce' (Lundby, 2009, p 15). In so doing, it places the media as the nexus between culture and society, as both policy shaper and implementer.

Although there has been little research into how it influences individual identities, there is a good deal of evidence regarding the ways in which public perceptions of social and professional groups are influenced and coloured by the media. Peter Golding and Sue Middleton's (1982) seminal work on *Images of welfare* showed how the press powerfully coloured public perceptions of poverty, while Peter Moray and Amina Yaqun (2011) have written at length about the ways in which media debates post-9/11 influenced the stereotyping and representation of Muslims. No chapter on the media and its influence on policy would be complete without mentioning the seminal work of Stuart Hall, Chas Critcher, Tony Jefferson, John Clarke and Brian Roberts on how the term 'mugging', 'hitherto used almost exclusively in an American context ... was affixed to a particular case [in Britain] and entered the crime reporter's vocabulary, shaping public opinion and policy' (Hall et al, 1978, p 1). These accounts of poverty, crime and religion foreground the very complex and powerful ways in which the media frames and articulates certain phenomena, manipulating them into entering the national consciousness and becoming eponyms for a range of conditions and, in many cases, justification for changes in policy.

As outlined earlier, the mediatisation of policy is not a new phenomenon; it is thought to have emerged as a result of a move from bureaucratic models of governing to networked forms of governance. There are many definitions of what the term 'governance' actually means, but, broadly speaking, it describes the 'dense sphere of independent, agencies, non-majoritarian institutions, "parastatal" or "satellite" bodies, extra governmental organisations, hybrids – "fringe" bodies, quangos [quasi-autonomous non-governmental organisations] … which have been created in most advanced liberal democracies in recent decades' (Flinders, 2008, p 3). Researchers such as Knut Lundby have examined how the demise of bureaucratic forms of governance and the concomitant rise of networked forms have given rise to new ways of policymaking – ways that are heavily reliant upon the media to form, shape and mediate them (Hajer, 2009; Lundby, 2009). This phenomenon is often operationalised by the use of 'independent' bodies to 'govern at arm's length', through influential bodies such as the Office for Standards in Education, Children's Services and Skills (Ofsted), described in Chapters One and Five and also by Clarke (2011) in his paper 'Governing schools at several distances'. The advantages of governing in this way are myriad, at least for governments, and include the restoration of public confidence in the wake of scandals and giving the appearance of a more disinterested form of accountability –'devoid' of and 'separate from' party-political agendas – to name but two (see Flinders, 2008, p 9). One of the key factors in this approach to governing is the ability of these quangos to work through the media in order not only to shape and influence policy, but equally to legitimise and give it professional and public credibility – a credibility that, in many cases, (but not always) transcends the electoral cycle (for a more detailed discussion, see Clarke, 2009).

Latterly, it has become evident that the study of mediatisation has become increasingly complex as new forms of social media infuse the spaces that were previously only occupied by formal media outlets. Innovations such as the 'Comment is free' section of *The Guardian* newspaper permit open forms of debate on any number of issues; however, the impact of such debate on policy is yet to be determined

(Singer and Ashman, 2009). Sites such as YouTube, Facebook and Twitter have changed the ways in which publics engage with the media, while also providing powerful channels of communication for policymakers and organisations. A particularly persuasive example of how this works in practice is evident in the ways in which Ofsted has nurtured and developed a very powerful online presence. This is articulated not only through its extensive website, but also via a number of social media channels (Baxter and Rönnberg, 2014). These media channels function as powerful distributors of information and policy and offer opportunities for publics to comment on and engage with the organisation and its mission.

Using a variety of discourse-analytic methods – particularly in relation to specific policies – some researchers have investigated the ways in which the complex interplay between policy and the media functions. Studies such as Sue Thomas's (2005) work in Queensland, Australia, followed a curriculum policy known as 'The Wiltshire Review', tracking media announcements and stories about the policy that occurred alongside its development. Mike Wallace's (1994) work on the mass media and education policy provides a powerful account of the ways in which the media shapes the policy process while also 'spinning' it via processes such as the de-contextualisation of policy announcements, for example 'feeding the media with soundbites', and other powerful techniques. More recent work by Bob Lingard and Shaun Rawolle (2004, p 256) investigates the cross-field effects of the media on policy innovation, and investigates what they see as 'structural amnesia' – the media's 'short memory' where the reporting of policy is concerned. They argue that reporting on policy frequently disregards any historical context and that this de-contextualising or parsing of policy from its historical and cultural roots is particularly prevalent when policy derives from political interventions (Lingard and Rawolle, 2004, p 367). In the same vein, Blackmore and Thomson's (2004, p 308) research into the creation of superstar heads suggested that the ones who mostly tend to be lionised by the media are those who are most closely aligned to government agendas. This is particularly interesting in the case of the Trojan Horse affair as, prior to the episode, the school at the very centre of the scandal had been lionised by the government and inspectorate as having achieved the type of progress that the government was seeking in all schools: good results in a deprived and multicultural area (Lepkowska, 2012). Sotiria Grek's work on policymaking across Europe looks at the wider than national context in terms of media influence, examining how the Programme for International Student Assessment (PISA) has been seized upon by the British press because of its story value and the very clear and visually attractive way in which it presents results (Grek, 2008), a phenomenon remarked upon by several reporters interviewed for this project (see later in this chapter).

A number of researchers have also looked at the ways in which policy is subject to 'spin' and the role of politicians in effecting this (Spitzer, 1993; Anderson, 2007). A particularly vivid account can be found in Dean (2013), who argues that recent developments in the so-called free press have gone so far as to threaten the very foundations of democracy in the UK. Research into the field of poverty and media representations by the Joseph Rowntree Foundation (McKendrick et al, 2008), in common with earlier work, found that media portrayals of poverty were influential when linked to a particular political ideology and were used to justify existing policy while also proving a catalyst for policy innovation.

In the UK, government manipulation of the media reached a climax during New Labour's term in office – a phenomenon summed up in a statement by former Prime Minister Tony Blair on his election as party leader: 'The only thing that matters now in this campaign is the media, the media, the media' (Dean, 2013, p 44). This focus on the media continued throughout the New Labour administration; its 32,000 press releases eventually resulted in a public inquiry, the Phillis review (Phillis, 2004). The review was prompted by the earlier *Mountfield Report* (Parliament, 1997), published in November 1997, which had

> identified a number of weaknesses with the existing system, including wide variation in the practice and effectiveness of press offices across departments. In some instances, there had been a

breakdown in effective co-ordination between civil service press officers and special advisers briefing the media. There had also been accusations of pre-emptive briefing by one department against another, and criticism from some senior journalists of the loss of impartial and press office service providing a function of record. (Mountfield, cited in Phillis, 2004, section 9)

Since then, the media has been dogged by a number of high-profile scandals. Yet, recent studies investigating how education policy is made and influenced suggest that despite recent attacks on the power of the media (such as the July 2011–November 2012 Leveson Inquiry [Leveson, Lord Justice, 2012]), it remains one of the most potent influences on education policymaking in the UK today (see Opfer, 2007; Perry et al, 2010; Bolsen and Leeper, 2013). Researchers in the broader field of communication studies have investigated the impact of the media on policymakers in some detail. For example, Bennett and Yanovitzky (2000) examined the patterns of congressional news media use and concluded that, 'on average, legislators spend 1.8 hours each day reading a daily newspaper'. However, other researchers believe that although policymakers are influenced by media, there is little likelihood that this will take precedence over their beliefs and ideologies, 'unless they are challenged by cogent contrary information' (Kingdon and Thurber, 1984; Yanovitzky, 2002). What form this 'cogent contrary information' takes is up for debate, particularly in terms of education journalism, which draws from a wide range of differing forms of evidence – some potentially less politically impartial than others (see later in this chapter).

The history of the development of the British press is complex, being riddled with political, social and economic battles waged against a background of both national and international news cultures. As Kevin Williams (2010, p 10) reports: 'newspapers mean different things to different people. Functions can be attributed to a wide variety of interests including: advertisers, readers, owners, editors, politicians, governments, amongst others'. Cultural theorists such as James Carey and Raymond Williams argue that the newspaper fulfils two very distinct functions: the first, the more overt function, is to transmit daily or weekly news; the second, a little less overt, but no less powerful a function, is to bring together the readership into the form of a community (Hall et al, 1978; Carey, 2008). This community functions as a powerful affiliation of 'like-minded individuals' whose political and ideological leanings can be used and targeted to frame stories by that particular media outlet.

Through the language they use, the agendas that drive them (their own and those of their editors and media magnates) and the sources that they tap into, the people who write the stories are influential in decreeing what makes for a good story, and what should be left to one side. The next section draws on data and insights gained during 15 interviews with journalists between March 2014 and June 2015, and examines some of the drivers and influences at play within their work and reporting on education policy.

Crafting the story: the journalist's tale

> The media do not invent social concerns, nor do they deliberately organise the priorities in public debate. But in particular periods of real social change they cut through popular uncertainties with a display of the political eternal verities around which social consensus is sustained. (Golding and Middleton, 1982, p 59)

The preceding quotation comes from a book on how the press influenced public thinking on welfare and poverty. Although it was written some time ago (and well before the dawn of social media and its influences), many of its assertions remain true. Golding and Middleton's work was interesting because much of the research took place during a period of austerity in the UK – the 1970s. In common with the period under scrutiny in this book, the 1970s produced a 'shrill and mounting antagonism to the welfare system and its clients' focused in particular on what Deacon (1978) has called 'scroungerphobia.'(Golding and Middleton, 1982, p 59). In a similar fashion, the current government uses the 'catch-all term' of 'austerity' in order to justify massive cuts to the welfare budget (see, eg, Golding and Middleton, 1982; Macmillan, 2011; Roberts et al, 2012; Meegan et al, 2014). Golding and Middleton describe three ways in which a story or image in the media (in this case, of welfare) becomes 'ideologically functional' – in other words, it becomes something that will trigger a point of interest for readers: attracting their attention and encouraging them to read on. They describe how the first phase will often be a precipitating event that 'sensitises' the media so that their surveillance procedures and journalistic categories are sharpened to 'capture subsequent events and give them a considerable prominence' (Golding and Middleton, 1982, p 60). The second phase involves a period that evokes 'a steady stream of previously latent mythologies about the problem which are then "dramatically uncovered" by the media' (Golding and Middleton, 1982, p 60). In the third and final phase, 'the legislative, administrative and possibly judicial responses to this cultural thrust reinforce its potency and provide a real shift in the structure of state responses to the definitions provided by the moral panic' (Golding and Middleton, 1982, p 60). These responses, in turn, provide news material and confirmation of the arrival of a new matter of concern on the political agenda.

This triadic manner of creating a story that will interest and engage readers has been remarked upon by a number of writers in the field of media analysis (see, eg, Stuart Hall et al, 1978; see also the creation of 'a crisis' mentioned earlier in this chapter). The creation of a media crisis in education and how it was used to justify policy change via the introduction of a voucher system has been written about extensively by Berliner and Biddle (1995). Their account of the Republican attack on US public schools describes how:

> The crisis was indirectly generated by escalating problems, both in the larger society and in education itself: but it was also promoted by specific groups of ideologues who were hostile to public schools and who wanted to divert attention from America's growing social problems. (Berliner and Biddle, 1995, p 343)

They also highlighted that one 'of the worst effects of the Manufactured Crisis was that it distracted Americans from the real problems of American education and from thinking about useful steps that we might take to resolve those problems' (Berliner and Biddle, 1995, p 344).

Crisis and its creation are undoubtedly very powerful political tools, but influences on journalistic reporting are many and varied and can just as easily reflect institutional and professional constraints as any political or ideological agenda – this does not mean that the two may not be inextricably intertwined. Entwistle and Sheldon (1999) identified several influences on health journalists. These included 'the constraints of news reporting, journalistic routines and journalists' individual role perceptions and values' (Entwistle and Sheldon, 1999, p 132). They also pointed out that 'the media relations activities of organisations and individuals with diverse agendas can also influence journalists' decisions about which issues and events to report and how to interpret and present them' (Entwistle and Sheldon, 1999, p 132).

Journalistic background can also play a part in what is reported and what is not. Estelle Morris, ex-Education Secretary and Patron of the Education Media Centre (EMC) – an organisation that aims to support journalists in their reporting of education by linking them to published research – explained what she saw as some of the issues around education reporting:

"A lot of journalists have had a similar sort of education background, that's why we don't get good coverage of the skills agenda and FE [Further Education], because the minority of them will follow that route. So we get an obsession with the Russell Group, because that's the background of the journalists.

When I was a minister, it was practically impossible to get a speech you'd made on FE into the newspapers. You make a speech or launch a document or a policy on Further Education or skills and it is really difficult to get coverage … on behaviour, literacy, numeracy in the media." (Estelle Morris, interview, October 2015)

Morris also identified what she saw as a particular 'partiality' when it comes to education reporting, something she terms 'the instinctively right':

> "Part of the problem with education policy is that you see something is instinctively right but it hasn't got an evidence base and the media go for what is instinctively right.... Homework and school uniform ... not much evidence that having a homework policy raises standards but you'd never get the press to buy into that because it is something that's 'instinctively right'. That is what we are trying to do at the Education Media Centre, collate evidence so that journalists can draw on this evidence. So, where do they get their ideas? Mostly from their own education, what they think is right."

All of this is not to say that reporting is the only factor that influences group and individual identities, and it would be naive to think that the press and media are the only factors that influence how school governors or any other body think about their role and function (for more on this, see Chapter Six). However, media influences are powerful and their policy effects undoubtedly impact on the personal and working lives of individuals (see Fink, 2004; Prokhovnik, 2005).

Interviews with national journalists carried out throughout 2015 went some way to exploring how journalists become 'sensitised' to particular aspects of education policy, and how these elements are picked up by other journalists who then run with the story. Their responses offered some indication of how a story quickly spreads as it is interpreted and reinterpreted by various news outlets within our 24-hour news culture. The following journalist goes some way to explaining why there is very little real 'independent' or, indeed, 'individual' reporting:

> "We have a media that is dominated by writer centre outlets, they are a prism – that they see the world in a certain way and the media will be influenced by them. Then, the rest of the media

influence the independent ones. Take an example from politics at the moment – all the writer centre newspapers are talking about the dangers of SNP [Scottish National Party]–Labour coalition – it is very hard for other independent outlets not to follow that agenda…. journalists are pack animals, editors are pack animals, going out on a limb is not as easy as you would think." (Journalist, interview, June 2015)

The 'sensitisation' referred to by Golding and Middleton is very often driven by editors or newspaper owners, who want to boost circulation – this determines what makes 'a good story' and what does not, as the following journalist, with many years of experience of education reporting, recounted:

"I was always painfully aware that if I wanted to lead a news bulletin, it had to be about X going on strike or the education secretary doing something radical and outrageous rather than what was actually happening in schools. Actually, one of the small circulation magazines that I write for now is called X and it's a genuinely education magazine and I find it quite refreshing because they are not interested in politics. It's quite a leap for me because I'm used to writing about it but they actually want to know what goes on in classrooms and how teachers are doing their job, which is very different from what most national education journalists write about." (Journalist, interview, March 2014)

One of the key influences on reporters is the way in which politicians issue news about particular policies. Hearkening back to the Blair era, Dean (2013, p, 34) describes how:

The Prime Minister's office has adapted to the 24-hour media cycle by centralising government power and deploying worldly-wise apparatchiks who are deft at 'spin' and 'shaping the narrative', these moves, a signal success under Tony Blair especially, have constituted both offence and defence in a public policy space that can all too easily degenerate into media tropes. (Dean, 2013, Location 131, Kindle edition)

According to one journalist, the relationship between education journalists and politicians has been very different under both the Coalition and the newly elected Conservative government:

"Blunkett – who became one of the key ministers – held a press conference every week for education correspondents; also, they [the government] had a good spin doctor, Conor Ryan, skilled at giving the media what they wanted.

[Today,] I think the climate has changed in terms of access to education policy – a picking of favourite journalists. Press officers have become a much less useful source of information, partly because of cuts and partly because of culture. Under Gove the culture of communication became quite difficult – he would brief friends in the media – that went on under New Labour, but not to that extent." (Journalist, interview, January 2015)

Education, it has often been said, is not an election winner in the UK, and this is often reflected in journalism by the hierarchies that influence who gets what coverage:

"It's part of the low status of education in the news hierarchy that politics and political correspondents have higher status than education.... Sometimes, the editors of newspapers will favour a story [on education] becoming a political story; it is a sign that there is not enough respect for the education correspondent. It is a bit of a symbol of how it can get downgraded, if it is a really important education story, it must really be a political story." (Education journalist, interview, June 2015)

As education correspondents tend, by the very nature of their work, to have a far greater in-depth knowledge of education than political correspondents, it stands to reason that the stories written by political correspondents are likely to link less to evidence and research – their focus being on the political nature of the story rather than its educational value. It is interesting to note that when the Trojan Horse story broke, many subsequent stories on the same theme appeared in the political, not education, sections of the nationals (although they also appeared there as well, sometimes slightly later).

There is a substantial amount of academic research on school governance, yet, in common with other education research, academic research on governing and, indeed, the wider field of education is not something, apart from a few notable exceptions, that has featured regularly in journalistic writing in the past. As Sue Littlemore, then Chief Executive of the EMC, explained:

> "The EMC was set up to address a slightly different issue – not so much a problem with the way research was being reported, but rather the fact it was hardly being included in education news at all. In my 15 years as an education correspondent, I rarely turned to academics for on- or off-the-record briefings compared with ministers, union reps, head teachers, who were much more accessible … in terms of their willingness to shift schedules to meet media deadlines…. My journalist colleagues in health, economics and science were, by contrast, in the habit of turning to their academic communities for comment and expert evidence." (Sue Littlemore, interview, June 2015)

Other journalists that I spoke to felt that academic research on education and school governance just did not lend itself to interpretation by the media, as the following correspondent explained when I asked why policy think tanks seem to attract more attention from the media than academic research:

> "You know what it's like … as a 'proper academic', you will have everything hedged around with caveats because you have to, and the think tank probably ignores a lot of those caveats and

just goes for the – they'll go in very hard on the policy angle. They will produce a report which really is a policy statement with evidence rather than evidence which might at some point drive you towards a policy conclusion. And with an academic report, it might not even point. As a journalist, you might have to interpret that and then go back to the academic and say, 'If I say that your work seems to point in this direction, what would you say?' Whereas a think tank would have told you that; it would be really upfront, because they would start from that point, so it's quite a different thing. It's very, very much more direct." (Education journalist, interview, November 2014)

All of the journalists interviewed felt that the influence of the Organisation for Economic Co-operation and Development (OECD) had been 'a game-changer' in terms of education policy reporting:

"I think that the key with PISA is that [they] just hand it to you on a plate. They work on that data to turn it into a message – it is so easy – it can tell you the story in a sentence – ministers, journalists love it." (Education journalist, interview, May 2014)

"There was a big panic in Germany about a decade ago and the way these things are reported is very much part of that, so you could argue that the media is almost a key player in the creation and development of policy. A less polite way of saying it is that politicians often react in a knee-jerk way to the way that particularly the most influential papers – that whole thing about how things like league tables and international comparisons are reported is really important." (Education journalist and ex-editor, interview, March 2014)

The reasons why these international comparisons are so seductive is that, in many ways, they come with the data 'ready packaged': they are large-scale and provide simple measures of comparison (Figazzolo, 2009). On the negative side, many argue that the data are not nuanced enough – that the comparators are 'a blunt instrument' or that the regime has driven statistics-based testing systems that are not always accurate reflections of what is really happening in schools (Ozga, 2011; Ozga et al, 2011). In terms of mediatisation, such large-scale indicators are very powerful drivers for education policy, not least because of the way in which their results are 'packaged' in order to maximise influence on national governments (Ozga et al, 2011, 2013; Pons, 2011).

It is clear from other work in this area that the influence of international comparisons is hegemonic within other cultures as well, as evidenced in the work referred to earlier of Berliner and Biddle (1995). They make the point very powerfully when they begin their book with what at first glance appears to be a list of what is wrong with US education: '[A] junior high school gang of six extorts $2,500 from 120 classmates, High school girls turn to prostitution for entertainment, curiosity and a source of revenue' (Berliner and Biddle, 1995, p 1), and so the list goes on. It is not until the second page that they inform us that these are all reports from the Japanese media. As they explain, this is all the more ironic as:

> After all, every week our media seem to supply us with yet another frightening story about the dreadful state of education in our country, in contrast, Americans regularly read and hear glowing reports of Japanese schools and their students' performance on international tests of achievement. (Berliner and Biddle, 1995, p 2)

They also argue that international comparisons rely heavily on what they term 'the legacy of Socrates' – that in rapidly changing cultures, it is highly unlikely that children will know what their parents know, and that parents and other adults may not stop to think that 'children may know different things than they do, a natural consequence of living in a rapidly changing culture with an exploding knowledge base. Their problem, like Socrates, is that they see differences as deficiencies, but such reasoning is questionable' (Berliner and Biddle, 1995, p 11). Berliner and Biddle (1995, p 11) conclude that each generation 'must determine which bits of knowledge from the past to retain and which to abandon in favour of new knowledge'.

In *The nature and origins of mass opinion*, John Zaller (1992) argues that the persuasiveness of an argument or story on a particular policy is dependent on the level of a person's political attentiveness, 'or to put it another way, politically inattentive persons will often be unaware of the implications of the persuasive communications they encounter, and so often end up "mistakenly" accepting them' (Zaller, 1992, p 45). Although this may sound like a reductionist view, it does go some way to explaining why news 'framing' is so important, as Phillip Converse argued as far back as 1964:

> Few people reason for themselves about how political ideas relate to one another. Rather, to the extent that individuals respond critically to the political ideas they encounter, they rely on contextual information from elites about how different ideas 'go together' [and] thereby 'constrain' [one another]. (Converse, 1964, p 22)

Work on the use of 'framing' in the media emerged largely via the work of Erving Goffman, a sociologist who began his career working in the film industry (see Goffman, 1959, 1974a, 1974b, 1981, 2008, 2009). His early work focused on the minutiae of conversation and interactions between individuals, and progressed to examining the ways in which media (film, news, etc) framed or presented stories in order to reach out to a particular readership, or presented stories in ways that engage. The idea of framing links to the ways in which stories are organised or framed within the context of *the existing experience and knowledge of the reader within that area*. It specifically includes the use of metaphor to create a consistent narrative between reports, stories and public understandings in order to create causal shifts in practices and policies (Goffman, 1974a). The idea of framing is very often linked to news values (see Negrine, 2013), and refers to the ways in which journalists attempt to craft their stories in order to reach out to the values of their known readership (see Baxter and Rönnberg, 2014). An important part of framing includes the metaphors that link particular arguments with an individual's experience and understanding, which are designed to deeply resonate with the individual reader. As Lakoff and Johnson (1999, p 118) put it: 'They [Metaphors] cut to the deepest questions of what we as human beings are and how we understand our everyday world'. Metaphors appeal to individuals on a very deep level and, for this reason, can elicit certain feelings that may not otherwise rise to the surface, even while reading a particularly emotive report. It is for this reason that they represent a powerful tool in the journalist's reporting armoury.

The next chapter investigates the changing media articulations of school governors within the period 2008–15. Using frames and the metaphors used within these frames, I examine the changes in the reporting of stories on school governance/school governors and explore some of the metaphors used to 'hook' the reader and to suggest certain portrayals of governors and their work. Taking four specific time periods – 2008–09, 2010–11, 2012–13 and 2014–15 – I discuss the changing nature of school governing across three key political periods: beginning with New Labour under Gordon Brown, moving through to the end of the Conservative–Liberal Democratic Coalition and, finally, at the dawn of a new Conservative government in May 2015.

FOUR
FRAMING THE WORK OF SCHOOL GOVERNORS, 2008–15

Introduction

As Chapter Three reflected, education is not a top priority for newspaper editors and stories on education are often squeezed out in order to give priority to areas such as health, social care or immigration. In terms of journalistic reporting, as one ex-education editor put it in May 2014: "[You] are more likely to find education reporters that are or have been school governors than have reported on it" – a fact borne out by this particular analysis.

Using the key search terms 'school governor' or 'school governors anywhere in the article' within the Lexis Nexis news database, and focusing on the category National Newspapers, I was interested to find that there had, indeed, been very few reports on school governors within the period 2008–09, with only 67 reports appearing in print and a mere 16 online. However, from 2010 onwards, this changed quite dramatically in terms of the number of print articles, with 249 appearing in print and 14 online. The period from 2012 to 2013 saw a drop in print-based articles (with only 98), combined with a substantial rise in online articles (121). However, the largest increase in both categories undoubtedly occurred within the final period under scrutiny, with 339 online and a huge rise in print articles that saw numbers rise to 749 (see Table 4.1). Taking each category in turn, this chapter looks to contextualise this reporting while also drawing on a sample from each period to take a more granular approach to investigating the changes in the ways in which school governing was framed during these periods.

Table 4.1: Articles on school governing/governors, 2008–15

Newspaper Print	Articles 2008–09	Articles 2010–11	Articles 2012–13	Articles 2014–15
The Guardian	27	74	18	97
Daily Mail and Mail on Sunday	6	33	6	38
The Daily Telegraph	7	29	6	56
The Times	9	19	34	43
Daily Mirror and Sunday Mirror	3	16	6	18
Sunday Telegraph	2	13	4	12
The Sun	4	11	3	13
Daily Express	0	10	2	19
Sunday Express	0	10	4	6
Financial Times	3	9	0	2
The Independent	3	9	2	12
The Sunday Times	3	9	8	18
Daily Star	0	2	0	1
Morning Star		2	2	
The Observer	0	2	3	1
Independent on Sunday	0	1	0	3
Total online	**Online 16**	**Online 14**	**Online 121**	**Online 410**
Total print	**67**	**249**	**98**	**339**
Total number of online and print articles in national newspapers	**83**	**263**	**219**	**749**

2008–09

The reports showed two distinct patterns of governor representation within the period under investigation. The first period from 2008 to the beginning of 2009 predominantly portrays governors as 'pillars of the community', often using the role as an add-on to bring a character to life – to reflect their standing or former standing in the community. Many of the articles make reference to an individual being (or having been) a school governor in cases where there has been some sort of transgression – a fall from grace. Such as this example from *The Sun* (30 August 2008), where a woman whose husband turned out to be a paedophile was reported as remarking: 'In the police station it was horror. I was a primary teacher and the chair of the school governors. My whole life has been dedicated to protecting children.' Or this case taken from *The Daily Telegraph* (5 February 2008), with the headline: 'A pillar of the community comes unstuck after a lifetime of public service: 82-year-old Frank Gibson suddenly found himself on the wrong side of the law. He talks to Elizabeth Grice about the resulting furore'.

This stereotyping is well recognised in media research. As Peter Morey and Amina Yaqin (2011, p 30) describe in their book *Framing Muslims*, 'the same old stories are constantly born and reborn from the constructed consensus shared within given speech communities'. Creating this kind of consensus, this 'cosiness' with the readership, is a powerful hook for the journalist, who hooks the reader into a new story via the use of the familiar. Lingard and Rawolle's (2004, p 256) 'structural amnesia' – the media's 'short memory' where reporting of policy is concerned – is interesting when considered alongside stereotyping because, in this case, the journalist relies on familiarity with the historical use of particular terms. So, although Lingard and Rawolle have a point in terms of the way media reports on policy are often devoid of historical context, the tools employed within reporting are designed to frame readers' understanding of what is about to be told and connect them with particular ideological positions or debates.

Sometimes, these tools will draw on historical debates on a particular subject, but the metaphors and language used to make these links will regularly influence a particular 'take' on the subject.

The work of Roland Barthes (2009, p 160) recognised stereotyping as just one of the techniques used to 'turn myth into form', placing myth at the centre of storytelling and placing storytelling firmly in the context of culture and ideology. This ideological basis of reporting relies upon the reader's understanding of the topic – this is based on certain assumptions that require little or no articulation in order for the reader to make sense of the work. An excellent example of this is given in the work of Entwistle and Sheldon (1999), writing about media coverage of the health service in 1999. In their study, they quote Best and colleagues who, writing in 1977, argued that the media reporting of health services was underpinned by three assumptions:

a) That the aims and practices of modern scientific medicine represent 'excellence' in health care and are central to progress in health.
b) That the production and consumption of health series are the principal means of promoting better health.
c) That because the National Health Service (NHS) is part of the public services sector of the economy, better health (more health services) depends on the creation of more 'wealth' in the market sector of the economy. (Best et al, 1977, pp 23–4, cited in Entwistle and Sheldon, 1999, p 119)

In a similar vein, analysing the sample of articles produced during this period, I would argue that reporting on governors within the period 2008–09 relied upon the public assumption that governors were:

- pillars of the community – not easily corruptible;
- 'good' people who were very often involved in a number of high-profile community actions; and
- volunteers whose work for education goes largely unsung.

Although there is little scope for gender analysis within this chapter, this is also an interesting area for consideration: the majority of the articles in the sample for this period referred to male school governors.

The myth of the school governor, premised on these assumptions, is used a great deal in these early articles to create a sensationalised story of how far the 'hero' can fall. In relying on the myth and public assumptions (created by earlier stories), the writers convey the sense that being a governor is antithetical to transgressions of any genre. This ideal of worthiness – a pillar of the community, an individual who should not be impugned, an aegis of robust character – is exemplified in this excerpt from the *Daily Mirror* (30 August 2009):

> VILLAGERS are boycotting a pub after its landlady refused to allow a poppy tray on her bar. RAF serviceman David Marchant claims she told him people could buy their poppies 'somewhere else'. But Bernice Walsh, 36, yesterday insisted there was not enough room on her bar for the tray to fit. Mr Marchant, 77, who is a parish councillor and school governor, said every other business he approached with a collection tray accepted.

However, towards the end of 2009, the reports began to change. A study by the Centre for British Teachers (CfBT), entitled *School governors and the new partnership arrangements* (CfBT, 2009), prompted a substantial shift in the way in which school governance was reported. The report, based on original research by Ranson of the Institute of Education, London, and Crouch of the University of Warwick, raised a number of serious questions for the future of school governing. Focusing on new partnership arrangements between schools, the study highlighted the dangers that threatened democratic models of school governance. Warwick Mansell (2009), investigative reporter writing for *The Guardian*, introduced his piece on the report under the provocative leader: 'Education: who's in charge here? A new report warns that school governors, traditionally amateurs holding professionals to account, are becoming powerless "pawns". Does it matter?'

The piece marked a shift in the way in which school governance (and governors) were framed: from being understood as models of probity and rectitude – stalwart representatives of the community – they became:

> Passive pawns in a larger game of power that was led by Whitehall with the local authority struggling on behalf of schools to retain something of their prevailing values … in exchange for the largesse of capital which they could not do without. In its conclusion, the report says the traditional stakeholder model of governance, with its roots firmly in local democratic accountability, is now 'beleaguered'. (Mansell, 2009)

This change in the media reporting of governance was influenced by a number of reports, both academic and produced by governor support organisations and the inspectorate. Among the most influential was *Using data, improving schools* by the Office for Standards in Education, Children's Services and Skills (Ofsted, 2008), a report which emphasised that not only should teachers be using data for evaluation purposes, but so should school governors. In 2009, Peter Matthews, an academic working with Ofsted, delivered a report which stressed that excellence in education was possible, even in the toughest and most deprived of areas. The report, *Twelve outstanding secondary schools excelling against the odds* (Matthews, 2009), was aimed at schools and written in a particularly persuasive style, not inconsistent with Vogler's (2007) classic plot architecture.

Inspired by the London Challenge – an outstandingly successful project launched in April 2003 and led by renowned educationalists that raised attainment in some of the capital's most deprived schools (for more information, see Woods and Brighouse, 2014) – the report strongly encouraged schools to raise aspirations, a factor that had been instrumental in raising standards in London. An earlier report from the Joseph Rowntree Foundation, *Schools governors and disadvantage* (Dean et al, 2007), had shown that schools in disadvantaged areas had most difficulty in recruiting good governors. This became one of the driving factors behind schools joining together to create federations governed by a single governing body (see Dean et al, 2007; Higham and Hopkins, 2007; Lindsay et al, 2007a; Chapman et al, 2009). Alongside (and, in part, prompted by) various reports on governance and schools more generally, Ofsted developed a new framework for inspection. Within this new framework, governors were judged under a number of very specific criteria, which included: monitoring the quality of learner experiences/outcomes; monitoring financial management (including value for money); procedures to ensure the accountability of the chief executive and senior post-holders; and compliance with legislative requirements, for example, safeguarding. Governors were also tasked with playing a major part in school self-evaluation (Ofsted, 2009).

New school structures, combined with performance measurement, were placing ever-greater pressures on school governance, as Janette Owen, writer of *The Guardian* Blog 'The governor', reported in her last blog post on 2 June 2009:

> Some of the themes may not have changed, but, oh boy, has life got a lot more complicated for the 350,000 of us who voluntarily give our time, expertise and energy to education. Schools have been bombarded with curriculum and exam changes, new Ofsted inspections, policy requirements, budget cuts, and more hoops to jump through than there are in a can of Heinz spaghetti hoops.

The rise in academic and government interest in school governing was increasing but reporting on governors was still not particularly popular with the press more generally, as Table 4.1 illustrates. The growing quantity of legislation directed at school governors was becoming onerous and difficult to keep up with, as reflected in Janette Owen's column. In response to precisely this type of issue in relation to head teachers, an earlier innovation had been set up in 2008 by the Training and Development Agency for Schools. This organisation (then called www.usethekey.org.uk) brought a new dimension to professional development, as Louise Tickle reported in *The Guardian* (19 February 2008):

> What does your desk look like? If you're a head, or on the school leadership team, it's probably buckling under the strain of paperwork. Being lumbered with bureaucracy isn't anything new, but senior teachers say it's a growing burden that takes up too much head space, never mind desk space, and they need help.
>
> Time to log on to your laptop – if you can locate it under the mess. Type in www.usethekey.org.uk, ask the nice computer a school-related question…. And you're through to a brave new world in which other people slog through a morass of government policy, academic research and other schools' best practice, then feed you a neatly digested précis of their findings which you can take or leave as you choose.

This new form of support was enthusiastically embraced by head teachers, one of whom sowed the seed of the idea of a service of this type for governors, too, as Tickle reported in the same article:

> 'It's going to take a bit of time to convince everyone in the leadership team to make the website their first port of call,' says Danny Moloney, head teacher at George Abbot School in Guildford, Surrey. But he's delighted at the suggestion floated by the Key's managing director, Fergal Roche that the website could be 'reskinned' with slightly different branding and marketing, and dedicated content could be made available to school governors. 'I would say there's almost more need for governors than for heads,' Moloney says.

However, during this period, other forms of media had sprung up to support governors, ones run by enthusiastic proponents of school governing keen to supersede the unpopular and fairly uninspiring government website, governornet.co.uk. An enterprising governor, Jack Black, set up his own website (www.ukgovernors.org), which published useful information on governing. Furthermore, at around the same time, the National Governors' Association (NGA) was establishing itself as an authority in governance and a major source of support for school governing. As Emma Knights, Chief Executive Officer (CEO) of the NGA, explained to me in June 2015:

> "The National Governors' Association (NGA) was formed on January 1st 2006, following a merger between the National Association of School Governors (NASG) and the National Governors' Council (NGC). The NGC was founded in 1994, with the NASG dating back even further to the 1970s (when it was known as the National Association of Governors and Managers). Members of both the NGC and NASG voted strongly in favour of the merger, which aimed to provide one strong voice and one port of call for all governors, giving governors a high-profile national membership organisation.
>
> Since its creation nearly ten years ago, membership of the NGA has grown exponetially – one in five governing boards in England are now NGA members." (NGA, by email, June 2015)

These developments would be instrumental in influencing media representations of governors from this period onwards.

2010–11

The period from 2010 to 2011 was one in which changes in school governing dramatically increased. Alongside this, press interest in school governing showed a considerable upturn, with a rise in both online and print-based articles in national media rising from 83 to 263 (see Table 4.1). The general election in 2010 had resulted in a coalition government made up of the Conservative Party (the majority party), led by David Cameron, who was to become prime minister, and the Liberal Democrat Party (the minority party), led by Nick Clegg, who was to become deputy prime minister. The election result was, in many ways, a surprise for all parties, marking as it did the end of

13 years of a New Labour government (Bowers, 2011). The changes within education during this period were almost unprecedented (see Chapter One). The beginning of this period was marked by the government White Paper *The importance of teaching* (DfE, 2010). In it, the government set out its vision for education, led by Secretary of State for Education Michael Gove. Gove, a talented journalist and former columnist for *The Times*, was close to Rupert Murdoch, the media magnate whom he has since described as 'One of the most impressive and significant figures of the last 50 years' (Addley, 2012; Leveson, Lord Justice, 2012). Always a contentious figure, Gove was known as being a passionate ideologue, whose strong opinions were never better exemplified than through his book *Celsius 7/7: How the West's policy of appeasement has provoked yet more fundamentalist terror – and what has to be done now* (Gove, 2006).

The government's ambitions, as laid out in the White Paper, included a radical reform of English schools and proposed legislation related to all aspects of teaching, from school leadership, pupil behaviour and curriculum and assessment, to the control of schools, accountability and funding, the setting up of free schools to be controlled by teachers and parents, and the expansion of the academies programme (for details, see Chapter One and Five). The changes to school and governor accountability were vast. Research into the role of governors reached new levels, being carried out by academics, government and Ofsted, as well as governor support organisations such as the NGA, whose report *What governing bodies should expect from schools and what school leaders should expect from governing bodies* (NGA, 2010) looked to iron out some of the challenges that were being experienced within this traditionally thorny area. Ofsted's (2011c) report 'School governance: learning from the best' set out exactly how the inspectorate imagined 'good governance'. This was accompanied by a report on how good governors could contribute to school improvement (Ofsted, 2011a). Meanwhile, the Cabinet Office (2011) was in the process of laying out its vision of the Big Society – one in which governors, as volunteers, were to take a central role – while, legislatively, the Academies Act 2010 and the Education Act 2011 set in motion the most substantial changes to the English education system since the Second World War, heralding a new era for school governance.

These changes invited a very different media take on governors, whose role began to be linked to detailed data, high expectations, financial management, accurate self-evaluation and power. The power of school governors had been under question for a while (as previously discussed), with reporting in 2008–09 reflecting what some saw as a diminution in their democratic role. In the period 2010 to 2011, however, the reporting framed them in a very different way, as this quote from the *Sunday Telegraph* (5 December 2010) highlights:

> A parent at the school, Fiona Kerr, said: 'We have lost the most fantastic head teacher, and for what? A few people's hurt feelings. It's disgraceful. The school had become lazy. Other schools had improved immensely and Devonport had stood still.'
>
> Miss Hill's friends say that the case raises important questions about the powers of school governors and about government reforms that would hand them even greater control. (Barrett, 2010)

The quote, taken from an article that described how governors suspended a head teacher, was, in effect, an aggressive attack on the power of school governors. The article used a particularly ludicrous example of governors 'abusing' their power in order to frame their increasing powers in a way so as to make them seem unworthy of the trust placed in them. The charges reported to have been levied against the head (framed as a hard-working and dedicated professional) described the myriad 'problems' that heads encounter in attempting to turn schools around. There 'should be' little doubt in the mind of the reader that both governors and teachers were complicit: first, in their self-interest (or producer interests – see Chapter Five); and, second, in being able to turn to 'powerful' governors whose interests were both banal and petty.

The article continues:

Within months she had begun an ambitious programme to turn around an institution that many parents believed had become 'lazy'. But little did she know that the biggest challenge for her would be the delicate nature of the staff.

When a slice of birthday cake was left in her in-tray by an office worker, she failed to eat it. The member of staff took offence and lodged a complaint with the governors.

The headmistress was also said to have failed to commiserate after the death of a staff member's dog.

She was further accused, wrongly, of confiscating a kettle from the staff room and another complaint centred on Miss Hill's failure to ask a colleague about her mother's health. (Barrett, 2010)

This single article exemplifies the changing role of governors – their increasing power – while also highlighting the 'incompetence of the local authority' – both themes that were to feature a great deal in policy at around that time. It also reflects central government's continuing battle to reduce the powers of the local education authority (LEA) (see Chapters One and Five) – a trend that had been on the agenda of successive Conservative-led governments since 1979.

2012–15

From 2010 to 2011, press interest in school governing was well and truly aroused, with some 968 articles searchable by the keywords 'school governor' or 'school governing', an increase of 622 articles from the previous period (2008–09). This increase came at a time when even more schools, particularly those deemed to be failing, were becoming academies (Easton, 2009; DfE, 2012). This took the total at the end of 2014 to 3,032 converter academies (including special and alternative provision), 1,264 sponsored academies and 252 free schools, making a total of 4,548 schools free of LEA control compared to 20,161 mainstream state-funded schools (21.6% of all schools are now free of LEA control) (DfE, 2014a).

As governors became increasingly responsible and their role became key in terms of accountability, the Department for Education (DfE) and Ofsted were becoming more concerned with how governors were performing in this role (DfE, 2011b; Ofsted, 2011b, 2011c). Other organisations were also concerned with school governance, and research was carried out not only into the role and function of school governors, but also into the models being used by the numerous federated structures that were appearing in the education landscape – multi-academy trusts (MATs), academy chains and hard federations (McCrone et al, 2011).

With the appointment of a new Her Majesty's Chief Inspector (HMCI), Sir Michael Wilshaw, in 2012, the inspectorate looked to make good governance central to the new inspection framework (Ofsted, 2012; see also Chapter Five). Government pressure on Ofsted had been increasing since the 2009 Programme for International Student Assessment (PISA) reports showed that education in England was lagging behind its Organisation for Economic Co-operation and Development (OECD) counterparts (OECD, 2010a, 2010b), a trend picked up by the press and reported in sensationalist terms. Ofsted was also under pressure to link its inspection processes to school improvement – previous research in this area had not so far found a clear link (Matthews and Sammons, 2004), and a number of research projects were investigating Ofsted's impact on improvement compared to its European counterparts (see Ehren and Visscher, 2008; Ehren and Swanborn, 2012). Meanwhile, in the academic world, research teams, such as that led by Chris James at the University of Bath, were conducting large-scale research into various facets of school governing – some of which reported that all was not rosy in the hitherto 'hidden world' of school governing (James et al, 2011, 2012, 2013).

Media reporting on school governance in the period immediately prior to 2014 was intense. Reporting focused on two key facets of the role: first, the volunteer status of governors, balanced with their increasing responsibilities; and, second, their capabilities, most often in relation to their key role and accountabilities. Previous reporting on the governor as a 'local worthy' became emblematic in the drive to convince the public of the idea that governors as volunteers were integral to the Big Society and yet, in many ways, not quite good enough for it, as this report in *The Observer* (15 July 2012) illustrates:

> For reasons that only the most self-effacing school governor with a mind like Occam's razor could hope to understand, big society proselytisers still repeat two words that, given the contrast with punishing welfare cuts, now enrage an initially sympathetic voluntary sector to the point that one respected activist, David Robinson, has just called the big society 'as much use as an ashtray on a motor bike'.
>
> Far from being strengthened in the first two years of big society, a new Rowntree Foundation report confirms, 'the voluntary sector is now facing an estimated cut in statutory funding of £3.3bn between 2010 and 2016'. But if that doesn't cut down on worthies, you have to ask: what will? ('Comment: Civic pride is alive and well – but no thanks to Cameron: Today its Britain's waterways. Tomorrow will our crime fighters and teachers be (underfunded) volunteers too?')

The incremental professionalisation of the governor role – a trend that had been emerging since 1988 (see Chapters One and Five) – was strongly reflected in reporting during the period 2012–15. Words such as 'professional', 'business', 'leadership', 'standards', 'results' and 'challenge' – all words that link strongly to a business representation – appeared with increasing regularity in the local and national press. Governors began to feature in articles that related to school failure and malpractice, a trend that has not gone unnoticed by governors themselves (Baxter, 2014c). Parliamentary scrutiny of the governor role drew attention to the very particular qualities required from the modern governor, but also reflected the challenges of these requirements in relation to the existing workforce (Carmichael and Wild, 2012; Parliament, 2012).

Press attention reached a new high in 2012 due to a number of issues. The first involved a more strident and active approach to governance from the inspectorate. The new HMCI, Sir Michael Wilshaw, was chosen for his background in turning round a very tough school in an area of high deprivation (see Chapter Five). For some time, the government had been convinced that the lack of progress in improving schools in deprived areas was largely down to a lack of aspiration and low expectations of pupils by teachers and heads in these schools. Sir Michael Wilshaw was well positioned to dispense with the 'myth' that historically linked deprivation with low attainment. His outstanding track record and 'no nonsense' attitude proved very appealing to the press, no less his habit of making provocative and combative statements about the 'sorry state of education', a trait that introduced a form of language into schools reporting that had not been witnessed since the days of the feared Chris Woodhead (Case et al, 2000).

Speaking out in public and in the press, the HMCI declared a 'war on poor governors', stressing that 'outstanding governance was key to a good school' (Wilshaw, 2012; see also Ofsted, 2013a). Government and press interest in school governing continued to grow alongside media interest, with the media now benefiting from vocal public figures such as Sir Michael Wilshaw and Michael Gove MP, both of whom spoke freely (and with regularity) to the press. Michael Wilshaw also used the increasingly influential Ofsted online media channels into which the inspectorate was pouring a great deal of resource and time (see Baxter and Rönnberg, 2014).

In a speech to the Freedom and Autonomy for Schools National Association Conference reported in *The Times* (6 July 2012), Michael Gove launched a bitter attack on school governors, branding them 'Local worthies seeking a badge of status and the chance to waffle about faddy issues' and going on to describe how 'More than 300,000 governors work as volunteers in Britain's primary and secondary schools. But too many sit on "sprawling committees with proliferating sub-committees" which fail to keep poor head teachers in check'.

In the same speech, Gove stated that:

> We all know what bad governance looks like…. Local worthies who see being a governor as a badge of status not a job of work.

> We cannot have a 21st-century education system with governance structures designed to suit 19th-century parochial church councils.

The speech, reported in all of the national newspapers, was infused with criticisms of governors as 'not professional enough', branding old ways of governing as 19th-century and many governors as 'amateurs'. Nonetheless, he was ready to champion the 'virtues' of the 'new governor' – 'the 21st-century governor' – who concentrates on:

> the essentials such as leadership, standards, teaching and behaviour.... [Whose] meetings are brief and focused; the papers they need to read are short, fact-packed and prepared in a timely way; they challenge the school leadership on results and hold the leadership and themselves responsible for securing higher standards year on year.

He also added that Ofsted inspectors would now assess how well governors hold their head teacher to account.

The comments provoked bitter retaliation in the letters sections of the national press. Ironically, most of these unwittingly reflected the language in Gove's original speech, and while many declared the speech unreasonably harsh, few disagreed with the notion that governors should be made more accountable, be better trained and adopt a 'more professional' attitude.[1]

Meanwhile, the NGA, led by Emma Knights, had grown in both strength and influence as a national voice for school governors. From this time onwards, Knights began to feature regularly in debates on school governing. From a reporting point of view, school governing was developing into a treasure trove of stories, with a now 'perfect triad' providing lively polemic: the professional head teacher and inspector, Sir Michael Wilshaw; the cabinet member, Michael Gove MP; and the 'voice of school governors', Emma Knights.

By now, the press was fully sensitised to the whole issue of school governors, and stories on all aspects of governance regularly featured in the national (and local) press. The language used to frame 'good' school governors was fully polarised and defined by terms such as 'professional', 'with high standards', 'rigorous', 'data-driven', 'accountable', 'no nonsense', 'clear thinking', 'strategic', 'businesslike' and skilled, while bad governance, drawing on terms used by both Gove and Wilshaw, described individuals as 'unprofessional', 'unskilled', 'lacking in strategic focus' and, perhaps worst of all, 'consumed by petty operational issues'.

On 4 July 2013, the Education Select Committee (ESC) published a substantial report into the role of governing bodies (ESC, 2013). The document, which ran to several hundred pages, contained evidence from schools, governors, unions and other stakeholder groups. Led by Graham Stuart MP, the ESC delivered several clear recommendations:

• A boost in governor performance including the introduction of professional clerks and more effective training for governors.
• Greater levels of recruitment from the business community with firms offering time off for governor duties.
• Clear standards now set within the inspection framework will help governing bodies to reflect on their own practice and identify areas for improvement. Where governance is poor or failing then the Government and Ofsted must act swiftly and decisively. Current interventions should be reinforced, including the imposition of time limits for implementation of an Interim Executive Board in a failing school. Greater powers for removing poor governors – including chairs – from office are also required.
• Payment for governors is not necessary, but there may be a case to consider remuneration in some cases – for example when governors deploy their skills or experience to disseminate best practice to improve governance in other schools. (ESC, 2013)

The push to 'professionalise' governors continued, backed up with numerous articles in the press about failed academies, financial mismanagement and misappropriation of taxpayers' money. In the period from 2010 to the end of 2013, no less than 347 articles focusing on school governance appeared in the print versions of the national press, while the number of online articles totalled 482. Many of the articles published within the period 2010–13 resonated with Golding and Middleton's (1982) description of 'a steady stream' of previously latent mythologies about the problem which are then 'dramatically uncovered' by the media.

These stories positioned school governing as an ideologically functional frame in which 'good governance' and 'bad governance' accounted for many stories about school failure. The language used in the reports during this period was highly combative, and in the same way as the 'battle for school standards' had been employed by the media as a means of framing the 'friend and enemy' of education, so the battle for good governance became emblematic for the ideologically 'slick, sharp, on the ball' business governor versus the 'bumbling, well-meaning throwback to yesteryear' type of governor that 'had no place' in modern governance.

However, at the same time that reports were polarising good governance versus bad, there was also a dawning awareness that recruiting governors – a task that had never been easy, particularly in areas of high deprivation – was becoming more difficult as more and more responsibilities fell upon the role (Francis, 2011). According to the media, it appeared that governors were regularly failing in their duties, a fact that was all the more concerning since academy governing bodies were directly accountable to the Education Secretary (see Chapter Five).

Until 2014, school governing was slow to enter into Golding and Middleton's third and final phase, a phase during which 'the legislative, administrative and possibly judicial responses to this cultural thrust reinforce its potency and provide a real shift in the structure of state responses to the definitions provided by the moral panic' (Golding and Middleton, 1982, p 18). While some legislative accommodations had been made in response to, for example, the report into school governing by the ESC, along with a more substantial inspection focus on governors as school leaders (see Chapter Five), by far the most palpable impact on legislation was primarily articulated via the change in focus on school governing within the Ofsted inspection framework.

Nonetheless, from mid-2012 until late 2013, the media provided the public with a constant 'drip feed' of governance stories in which governor failure featured as a central focus of interest. This set the stage for one of the biggest education media sensations of the decade: the Trojan Horse affair.

One of the key issues raised by the affair, as Chapters One to Four have illustrated, was the area of democratic accountability within the governance of schools, and the problems that occurred due to the rapid changes to the established system of education. In Chapter Five, I move to explore just how this system evolved against a backdrop of political and social change.

Note

[1.] See, for example: http://www.thetimes.co.uk/tto/opinion/letters/article3469258.ece

FIVE
DEMOCRATIC ACCOUNTABILITY: GOVERNORS IN A CHANGING SYSTEM

Introduction

As the previous chapters described, the lack of a proper and robust system of accountability and local oversight was thought to be one of the principal reasons why the Trojan Horse affair was allowed to gain such traction, and why it resulted in such a profound crisis for education and for school governance in England. School governing, as the Introduction to this book pointed out, does not operate in isolation, but has evolved according to social and political drivers forming part of a system of democratic accountability that has, over the years, mutated according to the dominant political ideology of the time. Changes in terms of what constitutes democratic accountability have also varied according to national and international policy drivers emerging in the field of education as part of a wider consensus on conceptualisations of both the state and society.

Ranson, writing in 2003, pointed out that 'accountability' is not an easy term to define, particularly in the context of education:

Teachers are accountable to governors and the Local Education Authority, but also to parents and students. Moreover the patterns of expectation and answerability are reciprocal. If teachers are required to account to parents about the progress of their children, they in turn can have legitimate expectations that carers reinforce the learning process. Such complexity denies any simple linearity of answerability. (Ranson, 2003, p 198)

In the same article, Ranson argues that the turning point in terms of educational accountability came about some time before the Education Reform Act 1988, in the guise of then Prime Minister James Callaghan's (1976) speech at Ruskin College, a speech that became famous for its passionate conviction regarding the necessity of a 'great debate' on education: a public debate about the whole purpose of education in terms of both the individual and the state. This speech represented the culmination of profound divisions between the government and the teaching profession over what constitutes a 'good education'. It also marked the beginning of what would become a government obsession with 'consumer interest', 'opening up public services to scrutiny' and 'customer responsiveness', elements of the New Public Management speak that came to dominate discourses on public services from around that time onwards (for more detail on this trend, see the Introduction).

'Accountability' in education is a multifaceted term. As Andrew Wilkins (2014) points out in his recent work on school governing and accountability, it is subject to a wide variety of interpretations. In this chapter, I explore accountability from the perspective of the governance of education, which necessarily examines how school governors are positioned and the roles into which they are inserted by the ideological and political changes occurring partly within education but also across the public services more broadly: how they function and fit within the broad range of actors, organisations and systems involved in governance. In order to do this, I begin with an introduction to accountability within the public services and continue by discussing how broader trends have impacted on school governance.

Democratic accountability in the public services: an overview

Conservative Prime Minister David Cameron, speaking at the Open University in Milton Keynes in 2009 and reported in *The Guardian* (25 May 2009), declared his intention to:

> Replace bureaucratic accountability with democratic accountability. Instead of central government targets and controls to make sure councils spend money wisely, we'll simply require councils to publish online details of all of their spending over £25,000.... This sweeping new power for local government will make it far more responsive to local concerns … these changes add up to a massive redistribution of power from central to local government.

He went on to describe how his proposals would also save money – an important factor during a time when the consequences of the recession were just beginning to bite (see Seager and Milner, 2009) – stating that: 'a useful by-product from this redistribution of power to individuals, neighbourhoods, local councils and cities, is that when you shift power to the bottom, you reduce the bills at the top'.

Cameron's drive to improve public sector management by creating greater levels of democratic accountability is one that has exercised successive governments since the beginning of the welfare state in 1944. The pressures of providing efficient services, free at the point of delivery, in the face of rising demand and periods of austerity have made public service reform a key priority in government manifestos over the last 50 years (King, 1987). As a result, the reforms that have underpinned successive government initiatives in this area have always been politicised and underpinned by the prevailing political ideology, combined with a need to reduce public spending and yet provide efficient, responsive and economically viable public services (Clarke and Newman, 1997).

Changes to public sector organisation and governance have also been driven by a number of factors featuring broader organisational trends emanating from the private sector: moves away from hierarchy and bureaucracy to more responsive, flat and flexible forms; and – as Cameron's speech reflects – a move away from bureaucracy to new forms of management inspired by 'the lexicon of new public management and neo-liberal ideals' (Morris and Farrell, 2007, p 576; see also Clarke, 2004).

As the Introduction to this book explains, the move away from bureaucratic forms of governing to more networked forms of governance more broadly has occurred on an international as well as a national scale. As a result of this, it has given rise to a more complex and dispersed system of organisations 'enjoying' so-called new freedoms from central government control. These freedoms range from financial autonomy to decisions on the shape and form of services (Clarke et al, 2000), and they have presented substantial problems of control for government, which continue to be resolved by new forms of accountability (Power, 1997a). One of the most fundamental elements within these changes is documented by Power in his work on the ways in which the processes and practices of financial auditing have come to be applied to many areas of the public service. In his book *The audit society* (Power, 1997b, p 3), he details how, during the late 1980s and early 1990s, 'A growing population of "auditees" began to experience a wave of formalized and detailed checking up on what they do'. This chapter looks at the growth of such regimes and their influence on governors and education more broadly.

The growth of accountability regimes

The change in accountability regimes over the last 25 years has been attributed to a number of elements. Newman and Clarke (2009) argue that neoliberal ideologies emanating from the private sector and the need to manage more complex mixed economies of care combined to create a more marketised system across the whole of the public sector.

As the Introduction to this book describes, the New Right conceptualisation of public sector employees – including teachers – tended to imagine them as untrustworthy and often ideologically motivated, and as being in need of 'strict control and accountability mechanisms' (Clarke et al, 2000, p 60). This idea gained currency following a report by the Adam Smith Institute, a right-wing think tank advocating free market and classic liberal ideas premised on public choice theory, which stated that 'producer capture – in the case of education the dominance of teachers and administrators – excluded the interests, views and choices of parents as "consumers" of education' (Adam Smith Institute, 1984). Disillusionment with educational standards was not confined to the Right, but also emanated from the Left, who were disappointed in the failure of the education system to achieve greater social equality.

The influence of New Right thinking, with its emphasis on public choice and responsiveness to public needs, led to the creation of a number of organisations designed to monitor or 'audit' public sector organisations alongside their local government partners. One of the most influential of these was the Audit Commission, an organisation that became fundamental not only in changing the ways in which public service organisations were managed, but also for changing conceptions of what counted as accountability (Power, 1997b).

The adaptation of the principles of audit to the management of the public services had a number of attractive elements for government, including its capacity to combine a sense of 'independent validation, efficiency, rationality, visibility … alongside the promise of control' (Power, 1994, p 92). The Audit Commission did not just appeal to government; over time, it became increasingly appealing to many public sector leaders who had initially rejected any idea of such a system being imposed on their own practices. The police were a case in point, as Duncan Campbell-Smith (2008, p 217) describes in his book *Follow the money*:

> They could see the quality of the work on offer.… The annual report [of the Audit Commission] showed that 'a close and collaborative relationship' had been built with it [the Audit Commission Liaison Group]. Its four chief constables had met

with the home team regularly and 'helped them with their enquiries'.

The incursion of the Audit Commission into the area of policing, education and, eventually, the National Health Service (NHS) was strongly influenced by the Value for Money (VFM) agenda. The VFM had begun life much earlier during the Labour government's 'Great crusade to expand Britain's welfare state' (Campbell-Smith, 2008, p 25) and the need to rein in local government spending.

However, the power and reach of the Audit Commission took another step forward in January 1988 when Margaret Thatcher announced her intention to 'Chair a fundamental review of the NHS, its current performance and possible alternatives to current structure and financing', stating that: 'We shall come forward with proposals for consultation and if they meet what people want, we shall translate them into legislation' (Campbell-Smith, 2008, p 255). Then Chancellor of the Exchequer John Major was instrumental in taking this forward – an important point to remember in light of his later work on accountability as prime minister (see 'the Citizen's Charter', discussed later in this chapter). The proposed role for the Audit Commission within the NHS was finally delivered in the form of a White Paper, *Working for patients* (Audit Commission, 1989), which was subsequently translated into the National Health Service and Community Care Act 1990.

As the earlier chapters of this book explained, the education system was far from immune from the influence of the Audit Commission and the new ways in which accountability was being conceptualised. Its critique of the education sector began in earnest with a report in 1988, *Surplus capacity in secondary schools* (Audit Commission, 1988a) which launched a highly critical attack on the lack of capacity of local education authorities (LEAs) to manage school places (Campbell-Smith, 2008, p 224). This was followed by a report that instructed LEAs as to how to go about delegating management authority to individual schools (following the Education Reform Act 1988 in which the legislation was implemented). The report, *Local management of schools:*

A note to local education authorities (Audit Commission, 1988b), sent one of the strongest messages yet about the lack of government trust in the capacity of LEAs to implement the new structures outlined in the Act. This lack of trust in LEAs, which began under Margaret Thatcher and continued under Prime Minister John Major in 1992, was fundamental in shaping education policy from this period onwards.

These reforms across the public services not only exerted a profound influence over the ways in which accountability was carried out, but also influenced the media and contributed to what was to become a 'national discourse' on accountability, articulated through the press and media alongside public consultations of one sort or another. Prevailing neoliberal market-based ideologies combined with VFM agendas to position the service user in the role of 'customer', a 'consumer of services' that, in common with any consumer, was entitled to both choice and value for money in the public services they consumed (Clarke et al, 2007).

The role of the service user: parent, patient, public

The trend to link education strongly with economic competitiveness from 1970 onwards placed increasing pressures on the education sector not only to perform, but also to demonstrate performance. It did this through league tables, the satisfaction of inspection criteria and a raft of other Specific, Measurable, Achievable, Realistic and Time-bound (SMART) measures designed to monitor performance, ensure value for money and convince the parent – as a consumer of education – that in the marketplace of education, their school was performing 'up there with the best of them' (see Ball, 2008).

The idea of the service user as a consumer took another leap forward during John Major's leadership from 1990 to 1997. Major came from a substantially different background to Thatcher, and his view of the public sector reflected this. Where Thatcher had been fully in favour of privatised public services, Major was keen to keep the public services public, but to reform them – make them more responsive to the service user and more agile in the ways in which they responded to public needs (Major, 1991).

As Major recounts, his inheritance in 1990 was 'unpromising', and public service reform was, for him, a prime focus for reform:

> We were on the eve of war. The economic bubble of the 1980s was bursting, inflation was approaching double figures. Interest rates were at 14%. Unemployment had begun to rise at about fifty thousand a month … the economy was in the first phase of acute recession.
>
> I wished to improve the performance of the public services. Where this could best be done in the private sector, I would privatise. Where not, I wished to devolve decision making so as to cut bureaucracy and improve the image of the service and the morale of public servants. There should be no excuse for poor performance. The culture of the public sector needed changing, and I believed I knew how to do it. (Major, 2000, location 4980, 4081)

Major saw his priorities as twofold:

> The first was the culture of the public services in Britain. Many of the services important to people were provided by the state sector, and funded by taxation. Despite many excellent public servants the service offered was often patronising and arrogant. Some officials seemed to have the attitude that as the service was 'free', everyone should be grateful for whatever they received, even if it was sloppy…. Yes although the public were wearied with poor service, they seemed disinclined to complain. It seemed pointless: the monolith would not listen … this perception was frustrating for the users of public services, and bad for the services themselves. (Major, 2000, location 4872)

The second major challenge was what he termed 'the political', which he described as 'the public face of the Conservative Party which carelessly sometimes tactlessly, still allowed itself to be seen as not caring about improving the public sector' (Major, 2000, location 4890). Dealing with these two problems resulted in a programme of action – the Citizen's Charter.

Major's key priority was education, of all the public services, he saw this as being most in need of reform: 'Our teachers and schools were saddled with a deposit of failed ideas and a complacent and bureaucratic department, which seemed to have a mania for expanding its authority and influence' (Major, 2000, location 4961). However, his belief that the privatisation of services was not the answer led him to look for a different way of solving what he saw as deeply entrenched issues that had proved intractable over the long term. In order to overcome these intractable problems within the public services, he believed that the resolution lay in publishing clear and unbiased performance data, as this quotation from his autobiography outlines:

> In fields where the introduction of true competition and choice was impractical, I was certain that publishing the performances of different schools, hospitals, local authorities or transport services would act as a kind of surrogate competition to raise standards. Those bodies seen to be underperforming would come under pressure to explain why, and to improve. If we could at the same time devolve more management responsibility to the local service level then local governors, teachers, managers, train operators and others would have the opportunity to improve standards as well as the incentive to do so. An information revolution would be just as effective a way of doing this as the left-wing device of regulation by the state. (Major, 2000, location 4968)

This idea of choice, backed by Major's information revolution, was enhanced by the imperatives introduced in the Education Reform Act 1988. The Act, which created Local Management of Schools, freeing them from local authority control, gave credence to the ideal of education as a marketplace and the need for the consumer (the parent) to be equipped with enough information to make an informed choice between schools (see Maclure, 1989). The Citizen's Charter, which led to the publishing of inspection reports and league tables, was perfectly in alignment with the ideologies introduced in the earlier Act and would change the face of school governing, inspection and educational accountability forever.

Educational accountability and the role of school governance, 1990–2015: New Public Management, accountability and inspection

As the economic optimism of the 1960s gave way to the pessimistic and formidable economic downturn of the 1970s, education became increasingly linked to economic success (or the reason for lack of economic competitiveness). The then Labour Education Minister Tony Crosland's growing dissatisfaction with progressive modes of education, epitomised by scandals such as the Tyndale affair (see Dale, 1981; Davis, 2002), was articulated within various papers and government reports that criticised the ideology of progressivism advocated by *The Plowden report* (Plowden, 1967), a document that endorsed and advocated child-centred approaches to education. The same report became synonymous with the rise of comprehensive education premised on the abolition of the contentious 11-plus exam, which in imposing certain standards on pupils aged 11, defined their future from then on. One of the most important outcomes of the report was the recognition that there were many deprived areas in which 'schools had poor buildings and equipment, matching the poor quality of housing, with large numbers of immigrant families, teachers who did not stay very long and often with low morale' (Lawton, 2005, p 73). These insights led to the allocation of £16 million to set up action research in five deprived areas and championed the idea of positive discrimination towards socio-economically deprived children in areas of high deprivation (Lawton, 2005, p 73).

The Plowden report, greeted with enthusiasm by so many teachers, was not so popular among the Right, whose vociferous ripostes were delivered in the form of a series of Black Papers that criticised the child-centred proposals contained within it. The debate soon became polarised: left-wingers supported the kind of teaching within the report; while those on the Right advocated a return to old didactic methods of education, the 11-plus exam and the old grammar school system – ideologies that underpin much of the right-wing discourses around education today. The move to positive discrimination was discredited during the economic austerity policies of the 1970s as part of a neoliberal ideological positioning that viewed socio-economic context as largely irrelevant to a school's ability to provide a good education for pupils – an ideal that would be taken up by Michael Gove, Conservative Education Secretary from 2010 to 2014.

The three major players in educational accountability – LEAs, Her Majesty's Inspectorate (HMI) and school governing bodies – would not emerge unscathed from these vicious and polemicised debates. The Education Act 1986, the Education (No 2) Act 1986 and the Education Reform Act 1988 all proposed sweeping changes to the ways in which schools were to be run and governed, and were framed according to the market principles that underpinned their proposals for reform.

A new approach to educational accountability

In common with other public services, the marketised approach, with less local oversight, required a different approach to accountability. Before 1992, all state schools in England were subject to inspection by HMI, which had been in existence since 1839. From its inception until the Education Act 1944, it had evolved in response to changes in the education system. However, the requirement in 1983 for all HMI reports to be published left the inspectorate open to far more public and government scrutiny than ever before, and led to increasing levels of government interest in their remit and function (Lawton and Gordon, 1987).

For some time, the government had become increasingly suspicious of HMI, which they saw as having too much power and being far too 'cosy' with the profession that it was tasked with inspecting (for a full account of this period, see Maclure, 2000). There was also substantial concern among the political Right that HMI had become increasingly aligned with the left-wing education agendas emanating from *The Plowden report* (see Lawton, 1979, 1994).

The creation of the Office for Standards in Education (Ofsted) was the government's response to this agenda. The new body, described by Major as 'The Parent's Friend', was designed to fulfil several functions. The first was to lay bare what had been referred to as 'the secret garden of education' – a term that had become synonymous with the progressive methods mentioned earlier. The second entailed dealing with the myriad elements contained within the Education Reform Act 1988, which, among other things, marketised the education system and offered schools the opportunity to become financially independent from their LEA. The third involved what Stuart Maclure (2000, p 72) termed 'the managerialism that had swept through the Government machine. Working patterns were reviewed and formalised with emphasis on targets and individual annual assessments.'

One of the key challenges for HMI had always been how to define '"educational quality", "levels of attainment", "quality of teaching and learning" and all the other elusive concepts which HMIs spent their lives pursuing' (Maclure, 2000, p 272). The emphasis placed on 'professional judgement' did not sit well with New Right conceptualisations of 'the professions', who looked to de-monopolise and disempower their so-called producer monopoly. One of the most potent of aphorisms for the difference between HMI and the new inspectorate is summed up by Maclure (2000, p 72): 'An HMI was more like a music critic than an analytical chemist. Judgements were formed from all the inspector saw and sensed as well as from the evidence presenting itself in objective form.'

This was not to say that HMI had no criteria – it had been developing the use of surveys and checklists since the late 1960s – but inspectors were reluctant to give advance warning to schools, feeling that 'Giving advance notice of "criteria" might have led teachers to draw the wrong conclusions – conclusions which could distort their behaviour as teachers' (Maclure, 2000, p 273). The economics of inspection were also a consideration at that time, as full-time permanent staff were expensive and it was clear that as its remit was expanded, it would be unable to cope on present levels of staffing. As Secretary of State for Education Kenneth Baker stated at the time:

> Once established the [national] curriculum will have to be inspected on a more regular basis than now. We will need a much enlarged national inspectorate. This will mean taking in to central government employment the local inspectors and advisers. (*The blueprint for education reform* [Baker, 1996, Appendix 2], cited in Maclure, 2000, p 287)

Eric Bolton, Senior Chief Inspector from 1983 to 1991, was charged with suggesting a new model for inspection. However, one of the key deciders came in the form of an Audit Commission (1989) report, *Assuring quality in education*:

> The report reviewed the mixture of advisory services and inspection provided by the LEAs, which now had some 2500 staff in these categories The report, while approving of performance indicators, still saw a need for inspectors to go into schools and observe teaching and learning. (Maclure, 2000, p 295).

The inception of Ofsted in 1992 was also a result of the Parent's Charter – one of the many offshoots of the Citizen's Charter, which viewed public services in terms of six key principles:

- Setting, monitoring and publication of explicit standards.
- Information for, and openness to, the service user.
- Choice where practicable, plus regular and systematic consultation with users.
- Courtesy and helpfulness,
- Well-publicised and easy-to-use complaints procedures,
- Value for money.

(Clarke, 2007, p 31)

Ofsted was designed to perform a service that would fulfil these criteria. It was designed to ensure that, via informed reports on schools, parents would be armed with much more information about schools and their performance. Through this information, they would be able to form an opinion as to whether the school was offering 'value for money'. In the provision of this wealth of information, the parent as consumer would be placed in a strong and informed position to choose an education provider that was best suited to their particular needs. In addition, Ofsted would provide the kind of 'arm's length' governance that could impose and shape government policy on education without supposedly being aligned to any left-wing agenda: they would not make the same 'mistakes' as HMI, nor be vulnerable to 'Inspector capture' – a process in which inspectors become too close to their inspectees (see Boyne et al 2002). The final chapter of this book looks in greater detail at this purported 'independence from government' and examines to what extent this is still true in 2015.

School governance and accountability

As this chapter has shown, school governance has been far from immune to the changes and trends across the public sector outlined earlier. School governors have formed part of successive government visions of volunteer participation (see the Introduction) and been a central feature of the democratic accountability within the context of education. More recently, they have been imagined and, to some extent, positioned as a quasi-professional body, capable of acting as a cost-effective middle tier of accountability in an increasingly centralised system of control (Wilkins, 2014; Baxter and Farrell, 2015). The ways in which governor identities have been coloured and conditioned by these influences and discourses are discussed in more detail in Chapter Six.

The radical changes to education brought about by the Education Reform Act 1988 introduced a national curriculum, centralised education by removing power from LEAs and greatly increased the powers of the secretary of state for education. They also impacted on school governance. LEAs, in common with the rest of local government, were accused of producer behaviours and the lack of a 'customer' or service-user focus. This effectively formed part of a polarising discourse in relation to the public versus private sector: a binary in which the public sector was seen to be sluggish, unresponsive to change, unwieldly and bureaucratic compared to a flexible, agile and innovative private sector (Clarke and Newman, 1997).

The increasing emphasis on school self-management through the introduction of Local Management of Schools fulfilled three purposes. It reflected the neoliberal turn adopted by many countries in an effort to find 'the right blend of state, market and democratic institutions to guarantee peace, inclusion, wellbeing and stability' (Harvey, 2005, p 10), and it gave schools the 'freedom' to innovate, effectively making schools accountable for their own budgets and spending – a move that reflected the VFM agenda mentioned earlier. These were all elements thought to be threatened by successive economic downturns in capitalist systems, such as those experienced during the 1970s in the UK (Lowe, 2002).

This combination of powerful political discourse and practical requirements resulting from school autonomy resulted in a far greater impetus for schools to engage governors from the business community. These governors were thought to bring 'ready-made' skills and a professional outlook to the realm of school governing. A guidance book for school governors produced at around this time stated that 'schools need to run like companies with the governing bodies being boards of directors and the head teachers the managing directors' (Thody, 1994, p 22).

The structure of governing bodies also changed, with more parents becoming involved and community governors being co-opted. However, Rosemary Deem and colleagues' research project into school governance and citizenship did not find that opening up school governing to a wider section of the population created the levels of democratic participation envisaged by the 1986 and 1988 Acts, as they explain in the following:

We found in our research that those with long-standing experience of citizenship activities such as school governance, namely white middle and upper class men, had not yielded much to members of more recently arrived groups. Thus although women governors made up over a third of the membership of our governing bodies, meetings and activities were organised as though the only outside commitment which counted was paid employment; childcare and the running of the household were not considered. Similarly, governors from ethnic minority groups were often overlooked for sub-committee membership. (Brehony, 1995, cited in Deem et al, 1995, p 97)

It was also clear that the changes to education had a profound impact not only on the role of governors, but also in terms of the amount of time that they would be expected to contribute to this volunteer role:

It was no longer enough to depend on the school itself (since to change this was the object of the reforms), and three meetings a year became woefully inadequate. Consumers of education or their agents were represented alongside those who were supposed to be political guardians of the production of education. (Deem, 1990, cited in Deem et al, 1995, p 95)

In addition, school governance still had what Bush (1989, cited in Deem et al, 1995, p 32) termed 'an evanescent quality'. Neither governor names nor turnover were recorded on a national register and governors came and went with little thought to succession planning, despite the clearly mounting levels of paperwork and the knowledge required for the role. The research also pointed out that, at around this time, there appeared to be a 'new emphasis on finance, human and physical resource management , surveillance of teachers' work practices through governor visits, entrepreneurial activity, markets and public/media relations' (Bush, 1989, cited in Deem et al, 1995, p,95).

These events in the history of governors have produced a schism in the discourse of good governance and accountability: on the one hand, the democratic stakeholder model in which volunteer governors are lay representatives of their school communities; and, on the other hand, and more recently, the more 'corporate' professional governor model, recruited largely for professional skills and abilities. In the final section of the chapter, I explore some of the tensions between these two models of governance and accountability.

Governors and inspection

The changes to education since the Education Reform Act 1988 have been substantial, as this account has illustrated. So, too, have the changes to the role of governors and the ways in which they are accountable – to parents, to the government and to the school. However, one of the most significant ways in which governor accountability has changed is in relation to the way they are inspected and positioned within the broader context of educational governance in England.

When Ofsted was set up in 1992, school governors were just beginning to feel the weight of their new responsibilities. Early versions of the inspection framework (Ofsted, 1993, 1995) were very clear on governor responsibilities. *The consolidated handbook for the inspection of schools* (Ofsted, 1994) was very specific in terms of what constituted a well-managed school. Governors were central to Ofsted's early vision of this and were expected to:

> Have a long term view of where the school should be heading.… Take a systematic approach to the analysis of the school's current and future situation. [That staff and governor] expectations are high and there are shared values and norms about learning, behaviour and relationships.
>
> That governors, head teacher and senior staff provide positive leadership which gives a clear direction to the school's work. That staff understand the role they are encouraged to play in the development and running of the school and also know that their contribution to the school is appreciated.

Clear objectives and policies, focused on pupils' needs are understood and implemented by staff and governors. The school development plan is a useful and effective tool.

Governors, staff, parents, pupils are clear about communication routes within the school and feel that these operate effectively.

Firm arrangements for periodic reviews exist. Performance in (or success criteria are used) and comparative information sought. Lessons learned are fed back to staff and governors and into the school's planning process and the school's goals are re-evaluated. (Ofsted, 1994, p 63, s 7.5)

The first inspection handbooks were, as Janet Maw's analysis illustrates, voluminous; for example, the 1994 handbook was around 300 pages long (Maw, 1995). The reasons behind this link back to the government's vision of the new inspectorate. HMI had been a part of the Department of Education and Skills (DES) but, notwithstanding this, it was intensely proud of its particular type of independence: no one could tamper with HMI reports, which were sent directly to the Secretary of State. They alone decided whether or not to publish them (Maclure, 2000). The new inspectorate was not just inspired by the Citizen's Charter, it was a test case in independent inspection:

The aficionados of the Charter made 'independence' into an overriding principle, a matter of dogma. They wanted the Inspectorate taken, physically, out of the DES and given a new identity as regulator and parents' watchdog. This would press home the ideology of independence. And to make the new status plain for all to see, they wanted the new HMCI [Her Majesty's Chief Inspector] to report directly to the Prime Minister. (Maclure, 2000, p 308)

The handbook was proof that the new education watchdog was transparent in its activities, that it was different from the approach of HMI, an approach that had been based around seemingly esoteric professional knowledge and shrouded in mystery. Ofsted would be both 'transparent and independent of government'. It would also be centralised in order to ensure that the LEAs relinquished even more of their powers (see Lawn et al, 2014), a thought that horrified some of the inspectors, as David Grant explains:

> There was a particularly chilling moment when District Inspectors were, in effect, told to throw away all their school and district files. Perhaps Ofsted would not want this material but the idea of disposing of such crucial local history in this way seemed appalling.… For me that was the moment when Her Majesty's Inspectorate ended. (David Grant, HMI, cited in Maclure, 2000, p 319)

Although the focus on school governing was very much to the fore in early versions of the School Inspection Framework, it began to take a far less prominent role as Ofsted developed and expanded its remit: first, in 2001, when it became responsible for inspecting all day-care and child-minding arrangements in England; and then, in 2005, when the Education Act 2005 set out the need to publish school inspection reports and to inspect LEAs. In 2007, the agency merged with the Adult Learning Inspectorate in order to provide a single inspectorate for all post-16 government-funded education, and it also assumed responsibility for the registration and inspection of all social care for children and for independent and maintained boarding schools (from a welfare perspective).

Although Ofsted was one of a number of inspectorates introduced in order to permit the state to steer rather than directly to 'govern at arm's length' (Flinders, 2008), the performance of governors themselves was largely controlled by legislation. Governors were inspected by Ofsted but the implications of a poor inspection were largely felt by school staff. Deem et al (1995) argue that rather than being volunteers in a democratic system, governors became what they term 'agents of the state at a distance' – individuals who carry out the work of the state without the 'political baggage' of a particular agenda, a trend mentioned earlier in this book.

Inspection and accountability today

Recent changes to the School Inspection Framework and accompanying speeches given by HMCI place emphasis on governors being able to strategically lead the school (Ofsted, 2012). As school leaders, school governors are measured on their ability to 'challenge and support the school' so that 'weaknesses are tackled decisively and statutory responsibilities met' (Ofsted, 2012, p 14, s 2). The 2012 framework – one that was declaredly far more rigorous than any of its predecessors (Wilshaw, 2012) – not only evaluated governors on their capacity to strategically lead the school, but also placed considerable emphasis on their ability to hold the senior leadership team to account.

A new framework, implemented in September 2015, was the result of months of public consultation (Ofsted, 2015a). The framework was accompanied by a booklet, *The future of education inspection: Understanding the changes* (Ofsted, 2015b). Within the explanatory document, governors, alongside heads and senior leadership teams, are held accountable in terms of the 'impact of leaders' work in developing and sustaining an ambitious culture and vision in the school' (Ofsted, 2015b, p 6), firmly placing governors at the very apex of educational standards and strategy. The new framework and the reasons why it came about are discussed more fully in Chapter Six.

For schools, governors and pupils, inspection stakes are high. Schools deemed to be failing may be subject to a number of actions at the instigation of the Department for Education (DfE) (Dominiczak, 2015). Culpability for school failure very often falls on the shoulders of the governing body, as a number of recent high-profile cases have shown (Paton, 2013). In these cases, the governing body is removed and replaced by an interim board. This board may have little connection to the local area and thus be unaware of a school's particular culture and context. Due to the high-stakes accountability of the role, schools are increasingly inclined to attempt to minimise risk by attempting to professionalise the governing body. In many cases, as this chapter has described, this is articulated through an emphasis on the professional background of the governor during the recruitment process. During recent interviews with governors, one chair described their recruitment process as follows:

> "It's a popular school, so we had a number of people come forward for the role [of governor], I interviewed them and in the case of one elected member, declined them because they didn't have the professional skill set we were looking for." (Chair of governors, interview, July 2015)

The School Governors One Stop Shop is a national charity set up in 1999 by the DfE to recruit volunteers with the transferable business and management skills to become school governors. According to Janet Scott, Interim Chief Executive Officer (CEO), since its inception, it has "recruited around 30 thousand governors" (Janet Scott, interview, May 2015). However, recruiting good governors is far from an easy task: both Ofsted and successive parliamentary committees have criticised standards of governance in many schools, stating that a combination of poor school knowledge, lack of strategic awareness and an inability to hold the head to account compromise the performance of schools. A parliamentary enquiry carried out in 2013 collected over 600 pages of evidence on school governance from governors, schools and other stakeholders (Parliament, 2013a, 2013b, 2013c) and concluded that there was confusion around the role and that standards of governing were subject to unacceptable variation.

As governor performance is largely measured by Ofsted inspections, it is important that the inspectorate understand the role in all its permutations and variations, but data from an ongoing study into governor identities found that within a sample of 221 school governors, taken in 2015, 59% agreed with the statement that Ofsted did not fully understand the role of school governors (Baxter, 2015a, 2015b). Following a statement published on 19 November 2015 in which Sir Michael Wilshaw announced his intent to carry out an 'in depth review of governance arrangements' (Wilshaw, 2015a), Emma Knights of the National Governors' Association (NGA) responded with this statement on its website:

While we welcome Ofsted's spotlight on governance, and enjoy a debate on governance, we do question whether Ofsted has the expertise in this area to conduct such a review themselves; their own school reports suggest that inspectors do not always understand the governance role and they frequently misunderstand the lines of accountability, almost invariably misidentifying the 'accountable authority' for schools in multi-academy trusts. (Knights, 2015)

In the statement, she also suggested that not only were the inspectorate rather lacking in a fine-grained understanding of governance, but that the ways in which they inspect governance should also be placed under scrutiny as part of their research, stating that:

Ofsted's lead HMI role for governance was unfilled for many months recently, and possibly as a result the inspectorate has been missing from the cutting edge discussions – as governance models for multi academy trusts have been developing. We would suggest the way in which Ofsted inspects governance should be included in the scope of this project, and we hope that as well as involving those who have the breadth and depth of governance knowledge in their upcoming survey evaluation, inspectors will soon receive the promised training on governance so that elementary mistakes do not keep appearing. The NGA looks forward to working with Ofsted in the coming months. (Knights, 2015)

It is fair to say that the changing nature of the governing role has, indeed, raised considerable challenges for the inspectorate, not only because of the changes in the nature of the role itself, but also because many of the 300,000 school governors took on the role in a very different political and economic climate, at a time when schools were more extensively supported by their LEAs and governor training was, in most cases, offered by these LEAs at a price that did not demand too great an incursion into the school budget. Today, in many cases, this support has been cut. Schools wishing to invest in the type of governor training needed to support the development of the extensive range of skills required for the role, in its current form, often need to buy it in at far greater cost than previously. The quality of such training was highlighted as a matter of concern in the 2013 Education Committee report into school governance (Parliament, 2013a, 2013b, 2013c), which concluded that it had a tendency to vacillate from the excellent to the execrable.

As explained in Chapter One of this book, school structures are also giving rise to new multi-level systems of school governing in which different levels of governance are giving rise to new roles and responsibilities. As one chair of governors working in a number of schools explained:

> "Whilst inspection of governors has improved (there was a real low point around three years ago), the language of inspection is not always accurate. When governance is split between, say, three or more bodies, inspection reports should reflect that. Very often, inspectors are holding governors to account in areas in which they have no responsibility whatsoever ... inspectors certainly need much more training on governance. (Chair of governors, interview, July 2015)

The danger of the present high-stakes, high-responsibility and high-accountability system is that many governors may well decide that despite the doubtless value of the role, it is simply too pressurised to fit in with an already busy, working, family life. There is ample evidence that time pressures continue to exercise even the most dedicated of governors: a recent survey carried out by the Key for School Governors (a governor support agency that specialises in answering governors' questions about the role) found that out of the 1,016 governors that responded to the question 'Why did you choose to become a governor?', 34% stated that they wanted to be involved in their child's school and 28% cited that they wanted to give something back to the community. However, the survey also indicated that the role requires considerable dedication: some 43.4% of governors surveyed stated that they spent between two and three days a month performing governing body duties, 25% spent four to seven days, and a further 19% spent more than seven days. Interviews with governors that took place between January 2014 and August 2015 revealed that out of 45 governors interviewed for the survey, all stated that time for the role was key to its successful execution (Baxter, 2015a)

The changes to the School Inspection Framework and accompanying speeches given by HMCI place emphasis on governors being able to strategically lead the school (Ofsted, 2012). As school leaders, school governors are measured on their ability to 'challenge and support the school' so that 'weaknesses are tackled decisively and statutory responsibilities met' (Ofsted, 2012, p 14, s 2). The previous framework published in 2009 judged the work of the governing body as just one element out of eight sub-judgements falling under the Leadership and Management section (Ofsted, 2012, p 14, s 2), articulating it as: '2. The effectiveness of the governing body in challenging and supporting the school so that weaknesses are tackled decisively and statutory responsibilities met.

In contrast, in section 58, the governors' role is specified as an integral part of school leadership:

Inspection examines the impact of all leaders, including those responsible for governance, and evaluates how efficiently and effectively the school is managed. In particular, inspection focuses on how effectively leadership and management at all levels promote improved teaching, as judged within the context of the school, and enable all pupils to overcome specific barriers to learning, for example through the effective use of the pupil premium. (Ofsted, 2012, p 19, s 58)

Under this framework, and because of the overarching judgement, it is far more difficult to see where staff duties end and governor duties begin – an issue that has exercised governors for some time now judging by the number of allegations of too great an operational interest and not enough strategic steering on their part (see, eg, DfE, 2011b; Carmichael and Wild, 2012).

Changes to inspection documentation were only one of a number of changes to the inspectorate's approach to inspection. In addition, accusations that schools judged to be satisfactory were failing to improve – that they were coasting – led to a change in the inspection judgements: outstanding, good, satisfactory and special measures became outstanding, good, *requires improvement* and special measures.

The change in terminology has meant that schools hitherto considered to be adequate are now the focus of more regular and stringent inspections (Ofsted, 2012). Since the Conservative government took power in 2015, Education Secretary Nicky Morgan MP has turned her attention to what she terms 'coasting schools'. Defined in the Education and Adoption Bill 2015 as schools that fail to ensure that 60% of their pupils achieve five good GCSE grades, this move is set to target many more schools (and governing bodies) for improvement, with many more potentially facing conversion to academy status. One of the central points for governing bodies will be contributing to the school's strategic plan for improvement. This will be examined by one of the eight regional schools commissioners, and if found to be lacking, will result in the possible removal of the governing body and conversion to academy status (DfE, 2015).

As this chapter has explained, school governors are central to the accountability and governance of the English education system. Yet, with more pressures than ever upon this volunteer body, combined with a still rapidly changing school system, it is clear that school (and governor) accountability is in a state of flux. The Trojan Horse affair, along with other similar instances of poor governance, have only served to highlight the challenges facing both the system and the schools themselves. Challenges to school governors are multifarious and leave no doubt that governors, perhaps now more than ever before, are first in the 'line of fire' when things go wrong.

There are also particular issues within certain areas: schools in areas of high socio-economic deprivation have traditionally struggled to recruit good governors, particularly those that come with the type of 'professional skills' judged to be needed by today's particular brand of governance (Balarin et al, 2008; James et al, 2011). In Chapter Six, I draw on recent research into school governance, exploring the roles and identities of governors in areas of high deprivation. The chapter discusses not only how they perceive their role, but also what motivates and engages them, their sources of resilience in the face of multiple challenges, and what this means for educational governance in England from 2015 onwards.

SIX
GOVERNORS MAKING SENSE OF THEIR WORK

> When organisational scandals occur, the common refrain among commentators is: 'where was the board in all this?' 'How could the directors not have known what was going on?' and 'Why didn't the board intervene?' (Hough et al, 2014, p 142)

Introduction

The changes to education policy that have gained pace since the Coalition government in 2010, as explained in previous chapters, have undoubtedly placed innumerable pressures on school governors: changing school structures; new complexities in networked and federation governance; and a system of accountability that places a great deal of pressure on governors to monitor school performance. However, these are far from the only pressures being placed on school governors today. As earlier chapters explained, the media also plays a considerable role by inciting opprobrium with sensationalised headlines that blame governors for school failure.

Rapid policy-driven changes have presented challenges for all schools, but in areas of high socio-economic deprivation – traditionally difficult areas for governing bodies to operate – these challenges have been magnified. Some of the most recent research into the challenges faced by governors in these areas is documented in a report by the

Joseph Rowntree Foundation (see Dean et al, 2007). Although the report also emphasises that many of the problems encountered by schools resonate with all governing bodies, it makes the point that governing bodies in these areas have particular issues:

> [Schools in areas of high socio-economic deprivation] tend to find themselves under greater pressure than their counterparts elsewhere.... to some extent this comes from the distinctive social, economic and educational issues in such areas – issues that manifest themselves in schools most obviously through low levels of attainment, and potentially high levels of special educational needs, student absence, student mobility and disciplinary problems. (Dean et al, 2007, p 6)

The report identified a number of issues that were particularly prevalent in these areas: difficulties in recruiting parent governors; difficulties in recruiting governors representative of the locality and socio-economic background of most of the pupils; difficulties in recruiting governors whose first language is not English, alongside suspicion among governors about the motives of fellow governors for taking on the role – particularly if these governors were from out of the area; and tensions between making governing body meetings enjoyable and the content accessible to most governors, and ensuring a balance between challenge and support.

The monitoring of non-financial performance, in the case of schools, the standards of teaching and learning, has also been singled out as a tricky area for school governors. It is by no means an area in which governing bodies in leafier suburbs are particularly confident either, as several large-scale studies have revealed (see, eg, Balarin et al, 2008; James et al, 2012, 2014). However, it is an area of particular concern for schools that struggle with low pupil attainment and the complex social factors that exist in deprived areas. The Dean report pointed to the difficulties in actually agreeing a common understanding of what is meant by '*service quality*', concluding that the lack of consensus within governing bodies often gives rise to problems within the areas of strategic leadership and the month-by-month monitoring of performance (Dean et al, 2007, p 37). This finding resonated with a similar report by the same organisation on the value added by community involvement in governance through local strategic partnerships (Maguire and Truscott, 2006).

Difficulties in monitoring non-financial performance are by no means confined to the education sector. Work on governance, particularly within third sector/non-profit organisations, has also highlighted the problems that non-specialists encounter when attempting to monitor non-financial performance (see, eg, Cornforth and Edwards, 1999; Cornforth, 2001, 2004). Research across this sector agrees that it is far less problematic for a board to look at profit and loss than to define and then evaluate whether a school is providing excellent standards of education.

A literature review by Perry and Francis (2010), which looked at closing the social class achievement gap for educational achievement, pointed to a number of factors facing families and governors living in deprived areas. One of the key concerns flagged up by the report was the need to raise aspirations and overcome scepticism about the role of education and schools. This also appeared in a number of initiatives launched around this time, including the Extra Mile (Primary) and Making Good Progress Pilot, among others.

However, a project carried out in 2011 using both large-scale survey material and 30 case studies carried out in areas of high deprivation (defined according to the Free School Meals Indicator) found that although there were difficulties in recruiting governors in areas of deprivation, the work carried out by governors was essentially the same as those working in more economically buoyant areas (James et al, 2011). However, this study also reported that the representation of local communities, in terms of ethnicity and culture, was poorer in areas of high deprivation (James et al, 2011, p 417), a finding also reflected in the work by Dean et al (2007), which found that in some schools in disadvantaged areas, between one quarter and one half of the governing body live outside the school's immediate locality.

Drawing on the work of Harris (Harris and Rochester, 2001), Chris Cornforth highlights some of the issues when recruiting governors from areas of high socio-economic deprivation: 'local organisations whose boards may not have the professional skills or experience to deal with risks and demands of increasingly commercialised environments' (Cornforth, 2004). Work carried out by Deem, Brehony and Heath (1995, p 37) on school governance found that due to recruitment issues in these areas, governors were often drawn out of the catchment area, resulting in 'Governors with very different social characteristics to the pupil/parent body, especially in those schools where pupils were from less privileged economic backgrounds or minority groups'.

The challenges posed by this lack of local representation appear to be compounded by wider issues around recruitment – issues that are even more acute in schools with low attainment (James et al, 2011, p 39). Unfortunately, there are no statistics available to show governor attrition rates in these areas but research carried out in deprived areas suggests that governors often struggle, for example, governors may be more prone to support leadership teams rather than challenge and hold them to account (Dean et al, 2007; Balarin et al, 2008; James et al, 2011). While these studies were carried out some time ago, they flag up areas that although by no means confined to governors in areas of high deprivation, do appear to be particularly problematic within such localities.

On a more positive note, a growing bank of international evidence suggests that many problems faced by individual schools – particularly in areas of deprivation – can be mitigated by schools working together (Wohlstetter et al, 2003; Chapman et al, 2009, 2010). These positive elements have been described in terms of: sharing best practice; economic benefits, such as centralised services and the ability to focus funds where most needed; increased and flexible staffing resources; and the opportunity to establish succession planning and retain good staff and governors who may otherwise have moved on (Baxter and Wise, 2013; NCTL, 2013). For a number of reasons, many schools are now choosing to work together, either in cooperatives, multi-academy trusts (MATs) or academy chain structures (see the Introduction to this book). According to research, these structures present both challenges and opportunities for governing bodies (see Ball, 2008; Ranson and Crouch, 2009; Chapman et al, 2010). The challenges are wide-ranging and include aspects such as difficulties in: communication with stakeholders and parents; understanding how to monitor a range of schools; managing large budgets; or deciding overarching strategy for all schools within a particular group.

Making sense of vast quantities of information, circulars, policy documents and statistics has been a feature of school governance for some time now. Governors are expected to be able not only to interpret these differing forms of data, but also to manipulate them and analyse them in order to hold schools and leadership teams to account.

A very recent survey carried out by the Key for School Governors (a governor support organisation) in 2015 revealed the emphasis that governors place on particular skills and attributes. Figure 6.1 illustrates that although 67% of respondents place financial expertise in first place, this is closely followed by the ability to build community relationships. Although the survey was relatively small, with responses by 1,320 school governors, the results were weighted by Ipsos MORI to match the population profile. The results demonstrated the continuing importance of the democratic representative role through the eyes of governors.

The same survey also revealed that, in their view, the top three challenges facing governors were: dealing with teacher workload (62%); teacher morale (49%); and governor recruitment (48%). In a summary of the kind of information governors were most interested in, the study revealed that governors (using the Key for School Governors support service) were more likely to view information and articles relating to strategy and improvement (24%) than in the previous year (19%) (Key for School Governors, 2015). The same survey also revealed that 33% of governors felt that they were ultimately responsible for addressing the problems if their school/s failed to deliver good standards of education. Although taken from a relatively small sample, these findings do illustrate that governors are keenly aware of their

Figure 6.1: Skills for a governing body

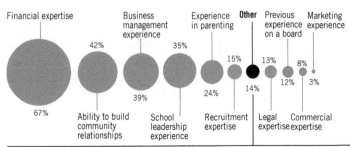

Financial expertise — 67%
Business management experience — 42%
Ability to build community relationships — 39%
Experience in parenting — 35%
School leadership experience — 24%
Other — 15%
Recruitment expertise — 14%
Previous experience on a board — 13%
Legal expertise — 12%
Marketing experience — 8%
Commercial expertise — 3%

What 'other' skills are considered important to have on a governing body?

health & safety, **public relations**, safeguarding expertise, **risk management**, data analysis, **time**, **passion**, common sense, **strategic planning**, human resources, negotiating, **analytical thinking**, team player, education knowledge, emotional intelligence, communication skills, **budget management**

Source: Reproduced with kind permission from the Key for School Governors (2015).

responsiblities, but while this may be true, they are also looking for more guidance in key areas such as strategy and school development.

This chapter takes Weick's (2001) model of sense-making in organisations to investigate how governors in three MATs are making sense of their working lives and organisations. As sense-making is a very important part of professional and working identities, the study also examines how these sense-making activities aid governor confidence and a sense of agency or professional empowerment, as well as what difficulties impede these processes and lead to governor attrition.

Making sense of it all

The ways in which individuals make sense of their working environments has challenged and interested those working in the field of organisation studies for some years now (Weick, 2001). A complex area, it links strongly with organisational learning (Agyris, 1999) and leadership succession planning (Bryson, 2011). Weick's (2001, p 39) work in this area suggests that:

> [Schools] have taken what is basically a two-person interaction between a teacher and a learner, and have added all kinds of tasks, responsibilities, and activities into this basic core relationship. Each item that is added represents a segment rather than an integrated part. Thus, there is no such thing as the school or a school ... therefore to refer to the school as a single organization is to miss most of how it functions.

This fragmentation of purpose makes it challenging to examine how governors make sense of their role in such organisations. Linking to accountability criteria is one way of approaching this complex area and has the advantage of breaking down the governor role into its component parts, examining areas that may prove to be problematic in terms of the governing function.

In order to explore what good governance looks like, Box 6.1 shows how the Office for Standards in Education, Children's Services and Skills (Ofsted) define an 'outstanding school', according to the revised (2015) framework. As the criteria suggest, governors are at the forefront of school leadership and have considerable responsibility for ensuring that the school functions well in all areas. There is also substantial emphasis on safeguarding – particularly when it comes to monitoring the curriculum and activities for signs of extreme religious views (for details, see later).

Box 6.1: Governor regulation

- Leaders and governors have created a culture that enables pupils and staff to excel. They are committed unwaveringly to setting high expectations for the conduct of pupils and staff. Relationships between staff and pupils are exemplary.

- Leaders and governors focus on consistently improving outcomes for all pupils, but especially for disadvantaged pupils. They are uncompromising in their ambition.
- The school's actions have secured substantial improvement in progress for disadvantaged pupils. Progress is rising across the curriculum, including in English and mathematics.
- Governors systematically challenge senior leaders so that the effective deployment of staff and resources, including the pupil premium and SEN [Special Educational Needs] funding, secures excellent outcomes for pupils. Governors do not shy away from challenging leaders about variations in outcomes for pupil groups, especially between disadvantaged and other pupils.
- Leaders and governors have a deep, accurate understanding of the school's effectiveness informed by the views of pupils, parents and staff. They use this to keep the school improving by focusing on the impact of their actions in key areas.
- Leaders and governors use incisive performance management that leads to professional development that encourages, challenges and supports teachers' improvement. Teaching is highly effective across the school.
- Staff reflect on and debate the way they teach. They feel deeply involved in their own professional development. Leaders have created a climate in which teachers are motivated and trusted to take risks and innovate in ways that are right for their pupils.
- The broad and balanced curriculum inspires pupils to learn.
- The range of subjects and courses helps pupils acquire knowledge, understanding and skills in all aspects of their education, including linguistic, mathematical, scientific, technical, human and social, physical and artistic learning.
- Pupils' spiritual, moral, social and cultural development and, within this, the promotion of fundamental British values, are at the heart of the school's work.
- Leaders promote equality of opportunity and diversity exceptionally well, for pupils and staff, so that the ethos and culture of the whole school counters any form of direct or indirect discriminatory behaviour. Leaders, staff and pupils do not tolerate prejudiced behaviour.
- Safeguarding is effective. Leaders and managers have created a culture of vigilance where pupils' welfare is actively promoted. Pupils are listened to and feel safe. Staff are trained to identify when a pupil may be at risk of neglect, abuse or exploitation and

they report their concerns. Leaders and staff work effectively with external partners to support pupils who are at risk or who are the subject of a multi-agency plan.

• Leaders work to protect pupils from radicalisation and extremism is exemplary. Leaders respond swiftly where pupils are vulnerable to these issues. High quality training develops staff's vigilance, confidence and competency to challenge pupils' views and encourage debate. (Ofsted, 2015, p 42)

As Box 6.1 demonstrates, the governor remit is wide-ranging and covers a number of different functions, all of which fall under the categories of strategic planning, monitoring of school performance (financial and non-financial) and engagement with key stakeholders. In the next part of this chapter, I examine how making sense of this role and its challenges link to strong governor identities, motivation and a sense of purpose.

Developing a governor identity: a way of making sense of the role and its challenges

The challenges that governors encounter during the course of their work not only form and shape their practices, but also exert a powerful influence on the ways in which they make sense of their role and assimilate it into their identities as individuals. A number of researchers into working and volunteer identities argue that developing a strong and effective working identity is vital in order for individuals to make sense of the working environment (Wenger, 1998; Weick, 2001): that it is precisely this ability to make sense of work that is directly correlated with both job satisfaction and resilience – an ongoing sense of motivation when the going gets tough (Nias, 1981; Reeve, 1992).

In the context of volunteering, these links are even more pronounced as intrinsic motivation (motivation linked to a personal sense of achievement and purpose) is not complemented by extrinsic factors (payment or incentivisation) (see, eg, Farrell et al, 1998; Hibbert et al, 2003). An interesting study carried out in Australia looked to develop an inventory in order to assess what motivates volunteers across the public services (Esmond et al, 2004), and researchers found that ability to make sense of their working environment emerged as a key element within volunteer motivation.

In order to begin to understand what motivates governors, it is important to look at the reasons why they decided to take on the role in the first place. Large-scale studies into school governance carried out by the University of Bath indicate that many governors come into the role for altruistic reasons (to make a difference, to give something back); others hope to learn more about education and how it works (Balarin et al, 2008; James et al, 2011, 2012, 2014). However, wider studies into motivation and attrition argue that initial motivation is not enough to prevent attrition: following their initial motivation to become involved in a particular type of work, individuals must then work to create identities that make sense of environments that often, following immersion, are perceived to be hostile and frequently difficult (Kingdon and Thurber, 1984). This finding is important when considering that governor attrition rates are purportedly high.[1]

It is precisely this tension that has prompted many identity researchers to view the formation of working identities as a process of struggle (Avis, 1999; Baxter, 2011c), one characterised by sense-making activities (Weick, 2001) and activities that involve the frequent questioning of role and function (Caravallo Johnson and Watson, 2004; Chreim et al, 2007). This process has also been portrayed as an ongoing struggle between initial perceptions and expectations of the role, and the role as it actually plays out in practice (Beijaard et al, 2004). There is also evidence to suggest that in order for volunteer identities to remain effective, the identities must be seamlessly integrated into other areas of the individual's life and work – that they must contribute something positive to an individual's sense of self (see Baxter, 2011a, 2011b, 2012).

Framework for sense-making: commitment as a form of identity formation

Karl Weick's work focuses largely on the ways in which people make sense of their environments and how this impacts on organisations. He sees sense-making as part of a flow in which searching for justifications for decisions is characterised as a basis for action. He argues that individuals form commitments around certain justifications and decisions; these then lead to decisions taken by the affiliated group, which, in turn, produce group identities and commitments. The merging of these group identities and commitments contribute to the formation of organisational identities and commitments (see Figure 6.2). In this way, sense-making contributes to both individual and organisational identities.

Figure 6.2: Sense-making as commitment

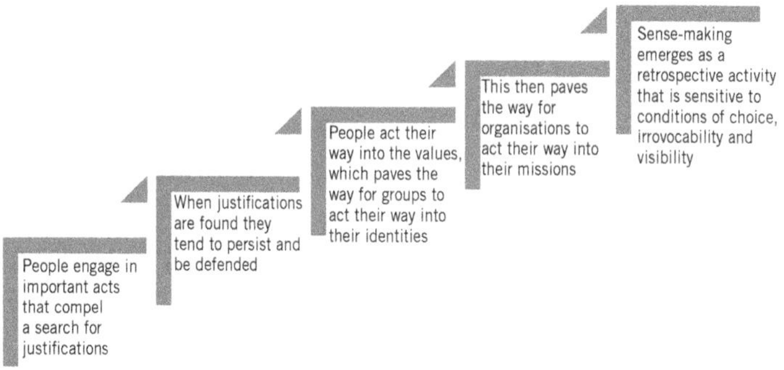

People engage in important acts that compel a search for justifications

When justifications are found they tend to persist and be defended

People act their way into the values, which paves the way for groups to act their way into their identities

This then paves the way for organisations to act their way into their missions

Sense-making emerges as a retrospective activity that is sensitive to conditions of choice, irrovocability and visibility

Exploring sense-making

Having established that sense-making is an important activity that links strongly to governor job satisfaction and the governor role within the wider organisation, I have adopted a case-study approach based upon a sample of two schools situated in areas of high socio-economic deprivation in order to explore:

- how governors are making sense of their role and purpose;
- what areas governors are finding most challenging; and
- what implications this has for governors in areas of deprivation.

Any research into school governance in England faces a number of challenges. The dispersed nature of schools (as well as sheer numbers – 21,000) and a lack of any governor records on the part of the Department for Education (DfE) in terms of numbers, ethnicity, gender or attrition rates make this a difficult field to research. Large-scale quantitative studies are useful in order to identify broad trends, but often fail to penetrate single issues at local levels (Deem and Brehony, 1994). A number of research projects into school governance have proved that more nuanced investigations are better achieved with a case-study approach (see, eg, Deem et al, 1995; Ranson et al, 2005; Wilkins, 2014), and some of the most comprehensive studies use a combination of the two (James et al, 2011, 2012). This study was designed to produce deep insights into the working lives of governors, and for this reason, a large-scale survey method was not used.

Governors self-selected and were interviewed both within their schools and off the premises, depending upon their choice. The interviews lasted approximately one hour each and were semi-structured, taking a phenomenological approach that permitted them to tell their stories about how they made sense of their work (Schütz, 1967; Husserl, 1997). This approach has proved to be successful in identity research in allowing participants to place their own emphasis on areas that they feel to be important to them in narrativising personal accounts of sense-making activities (see, eg, Avis, 1999; Baxter, 2004; Baxter and Wise, 2013). My previous work into professional and personal identities indicates that in the process of constructing a narrative of their experience and lives, they also construct a powerful narrative of their identity – the way in which they see and position themselves in particular situations (Baxter, 2011a, 2011b, 2011c, 2012, 2013; Baxter and Wise, 2013).

Weick's framework for sense-making has been used effectively in work on third sector boards in order to see how boards' monitoring and judgement processes develop and change (Hough et al, 2014). In other contexts, it has been widely applied to examine recruitment and retention in complex organisations and to help to understand how people make decisions that may not always be appropriate to the context in which they are placed (Patriotta, 2003; Weick et al, 2005).

This study employs a form of this framework in order to investigate how governors make sense of non-financial performance and to investigate areas of difficulty in their role as governors in areas of high socio-economic deprivation. The rationale for focusing on non-financial monitoring is guided by the work of Hough et al (2014, p 142), who argue that 'While financial monitoring is dominated by the routines of financial reporting and comparison with budgets or historic performance, greatly aided by money as a common unit of measure, the mechanisms of monitoring non-financial performance are less well established'.

The ways in which governors are expected to monitor the non-financial performance of schools have developed over a number of years. This is partly due to various iterations of the inspection frameworks (see Chapter Five), and partly in response to an incremental rise in the use of performance data in the measurement of educational outcomes (Ozga, 2009; Ozga et al, 2011). *The importance of teaching: The Schools White Paper 2010* (DfE, 2010) rationalises this placing of 'far more information into the public domain' in terms of making it easier to: 'understand a school's performance more fully; place expenditure information online; reform performance tables so that they set out our high expectations; [and] institute a new measure of how well deprived pupils do' (DfE, 2010, p.13).

A great deal of this quantitative data is now expected to be used by governors in order to monitor and evaluate their school's performance. Innovations such as Ofsted's data dashboard and intensive training sessions on the school data management system (RAISEonline) all aim to ensure that governors are well informed about their own school performance and capable of independently verifying how it compares to other schools, both in the area and nationally. However, quantitative data is not the only means by which governors are expected to monitor performance. *The governance handbook* (DfE, 2015b, section 2.4.3.45, School Visits) states that:

> Governors need to know their school if accountability is going to be robust and their vision for the school is to be achieved. Many governors find that visiting, particularly during the day, is a helpful way to find out more about the school. Through prearranged visits that have a clear focus, governors can see for themselves whether the school is implementing their policies and improvement plans and how they are working in practice. Visits also provide an opportunity to talk with pupils, staff and parents to gather their views, though are unlikely to be sufficient for these purposes.

Both Ofsted and the DfE also stress the need for governors to be aware of the limitations of their role. The same guidance states that:

> Governors are not inspectors and it is not their role to assess the quality or method of teaching or extent of learning. They are also not school managers and should make sure they do not interfere in the day-to-day running of the school. Both are the role of the headteacher. If governors wish to spend time within a classroom, they need to be very clear why they are doing so (DfE, 2015b, section 2.4.3.45, School Visits)

Trustees and governors overstepping the boundary between governance and management (the strategic and the operational) is well documented in the literature on school governing (Farrell, 2005; DfE, 2011b), and many governors interviewed for this study felt that the increasing emphasis on professional governors was exacerbating this tendency, often at the expense of concentrating on important governing business such as strategy, as this chair of governors reported:

> "Only through a lot of experience of being there, when I started governing, both boards were not very strategically aware, the

school I am at now, there was no strategic focus until a couple of years ago. I don't think the way governance has been put together, it doesn't lend itself to strategic thinking. In business, it's obvious you are deciding what the strategy is going to be, you are going to conquer America. What's to strategise in schools, they are all doing the same thing, aren't they?" (Chair of governors, interview, May 2014)

Hough and colleagues, writing about not-for-profit boards, point out that there are both cognitive and technical reasons why monitoring non-financial performance may be challenging. One of the reasons uncovered by research in this area is that the cognitive element of sense-making centres upon the idea of governors' use of schemata or cognitive framing in order to make sense of complex environments. More generally, this is the idea that individuals accept some information and reject other information (that may be equally valid) should it fail to fit with their world view or existing understandings of a phenomenon (Goffman, 1974a). According to this theory, in an attempt to gain a rapid understanding of a field outside of their own realm of expertise, governors frequently end up failing to measure what matters, reverting instead to measuring what is easiest to measure (Neely, 2002).

This focus on measuring what is easy is, according to some governors, is also partly due to the lack of strategic focus of some boards, as one governor explains here:

"You need to know what is going on over the course of the year, sure, but the most important thing is the view of where we want to be in three or four years' time, there is no training on that and 'cos most teacher governors are focused on the detail, getting them to think more strategically is a challenge. Things that are done jointly, heads with governors – seeing each other's contribution and getting a clear view of where governance ends and where management begins – would be an ideal way forward for governor training." (Chair of governors, interview, July 2015)

Reports and research into how school governors come by their information point out that, in some cases, particularly in the case of failing schools, head teachers and senior leadership teams have sometimes misled governors, presenting rosy accounts of teaching, learning and attainment that bear little resemblance to reality (Balarin et al, 2008; Ofsted, 2011a; James et al, 2012). To some extent, Ofsted's data dashboard (which provides school data in an easily accessible graphically illustrated form), along with a heightened focus on data analysis training, have tried to combat this in an attempt to provide an unmediated view of school performance.

The setting

The project is based on a qualitative case study set in two areas of high deprivation (based on above-average free school meals entitlement). The sample was based in two MATs. Academies are independent state-funded schools that receive their funding directly from central government, rather than through a local education authority (LEA). They have more freedom than LEA schools over their budget, curriculum, length of terms and school days, and are not obliged to follow national pay and conditions for teachers.

MATs are composed of groups of academies governed by a single trust. The trust consists of members (of the trust) and trustees. The members are akin to shareholders of a company; they have ultimate control over the trust, the ability to appoint some of the trustees and the right to amend the trust's articles of association. The trustees 'are responsible for the same three core governance functions performed by the governing body in a maintained school: setting the strategic direction of the school; holding the senior leadership team to account; and ensuring financial probity' (NCTL, 2013, p 4). As charity trustees, they must also ensure that they comply with charity law requirements – academy trusts are charitable companies and the trustees are the company directors and must comply with company law. Local governing bodies comprise individuals who sit on the governing bodies of each school. They may or may not also be trustees; often, the chair of a local governing body is also a trustee and they may have more or less decision-making and financial power depending upon how much of this power has been delegated to them by the trust. Some local governing bodies are termed 'advisory bodies' in cases where they have no decision-making or financial powers (NCTL, 2013).

The schools in this sample are located in areas of high deprivation according to the English Indices of Deprivation, a tool that identifies areas of relative deprivation for England in which each area is awarded a rank from the most to least deprived in the country, and both are located in areas that feature in the most deprived 30% of all Lower Layer Super Output Areas (LSOAs) in England.

The first group of schools takes the form of a MAT. It provides education for pupils aged 2–19 and comprises five academies. Academies one to three share the same campus. Academies four and five are located in different parts of the same town. The trust operates a single distributed leadership model, with one chief executive, an executive director and a principal for each academy.

The school is governed by a board of directors (nine in total) and three local governing bodies. One body governs schools one to three (see later) (20 members), one governs academy four (10 members) and the third body governs the special school (six members). Some directors also sit on local governing bodies or have done so in the past.

The second federation is a trust formed seven years ago. The federation consists of five schools: two first schools (pupils aged 5–8), two middle schools (pupils aged 9–13) and a secondary school (pupils aged 13–18). The schools are all within the same town, although none of them share a campus. The trust was set up in order to provide continuity for pupils throughout the three stages of their education. Governance is organised within two tiers, with governors forming a board of trustees and linking with individual local governing bodies at each school. The federation's Ofsted judgements range from 'requires improvement' to 'good', with four out of the five schools being judged as good and one requiring improvement. Again, some trustees also sit on local school governing bodies.

Analysing the responses

Figure 6.3 illustrates facets of sense–making activities used as a framework for analysing governor responses.

Figure 6.3: Elements of sense-making

7. Justifications are not fully formed immediately after commitment occurs. They are worked out over time as the implications of the action are gradually discovered and new meanings of the action are created

6. Post-education behaviour differs from pre-decision behaviour. During pre-decision period, people pay equal attention to alternatives in an effort to reduce their ignorance. If there is differential attention to alternatives, they pay more attention to the alternatives they eventually reject (Daft and lengel, 1986)

1. Sense-making is focused around actions around which the strongest commitments form

THE GOVERNER

2. Sense-making consists of justifications that are advocated and sanctioned by reference groups with which the actors identify

5. Metaphors can help to link old meanings with new

4. New justifications and meanings are slow to emerge as they are grounded in old meanings and justifications that persist even if outdated. Organisational life may be experienced as empty and meaningless – sense of anomie should decline the more committing to the context in which action takes place

3. Actions come to mean whatever justification is attached to them

Examining the work of the school governor in light of Weick's assertions offers some interesting insights into the ways in which school governors make sense of their environment. It also offers some insight into the challenges that they are facing and how they are attempting to overcome them.

In terms of governor monitoring of school performance, it appears that, according to this model, governors gain more confidence in their monitoring processes (correct or not) if those monitoring processes are carried out in a highly visible way. The reasoning behind this is that in situations in which this decision-making is highly visible, it is more important for them to emphatically justify why they took this particular course of action (point 1 in Figure 6.3).

Point 2 in Figure 6.3 indicates that sense-making consists of justifications that are advocated and sanctioned by reference groups that are important to governors. Which groups are most influential to governors goes some way to explaining why information presented by the head teacher and senior leadership team may be profoundly influential in governors' monitoring processes, while also raising questions as to the extent to which externally offered data on school performance actually influences governor opinions on school performance (compared to that offered by a powerful reference group).

Point 4 in Figure 6.3 goes some way to explaining why governors may find new regulatory accountabilities difficult to adopt as robust governor identities are very likely to be rooted in old meanings and justifications – meanings that align with governor purpose and identity. It also suggests that too abrupt and swift an imposition of such regulatory elements may lead to a sense of governor alienation or anomie unless governors are allowed to explore the implications of monitoring these new elements and can become committed to justifying them.

Challenges and opportunities

Analysis of the interviews placed governor sense-making activities into eight broad areas:

- making sense of context;
- the federation structure;
- previous governing experience;
- areas of difficulty;
- Ofsted and accountability;

- strategic contributions; and
- feelings on the role and efficiency in this role – doing a good job.

Making sense of context

Governors were very much aware of the context in which they were working. They were very aware of their school's history and the role played by the school within the local community. The following governor described how the school's façade often hid the real challenges faced by students, governors and teachers in that area:

> "This is a really tough area … we could go right around all of the five schools [in the federation] and you would see some signs of quality, which makes you think, well this school is doing alright, but it is very tough here and sometimes the façade hides the reality, it really does." (Governor trustee, interview, August 2014)

The use of metaphor featured in some of the very vivid descriptions that governors used to convey the sense of the tough areas in which they worked. At times, these were used in a negative sense to stress the tough nature of the school and to link this to the hard work and struggle that they felt was part of their role. However, many also used powerful anecdotes to convey the very strong community support that they felt was present in their school:

> "I went to the Christmas concert and you could have been in a Working Men's Club; cigarette smoke, ash and smell just wafted through the school hall and they came out in force – the support for the children is absolutely incredible, and you look around the hall and you think … yes this is a deprived area – you forget sometimes." (Governor trustee and local group 2 member, interview, May 2014)

There were mixed feelings about what some governors felt to be unfair perceptions with regard to low aspiration and poor teaching in their schools – a number made frequent reference to Ofsted judgements and reporting in the media around school inspections. The following governor in particular felt that reporting in the media on Ofsted judgements made a hard job even harder:

> "When teachers have low aspirations, they are the ones that are not doing a good job, they are the ones needing improvement and should be judged inadequate [in Ofsted and media reporting]. It is a bit of a slight against all of the outstanding teachers who work in these areas." (Governor and local group member, interview, May 2014)

Another felt that working in deprived areas was often misunderstood by inspectors:

> "It's an argument that is given by somebody who hasn't worked in an area like this. It is a constant battle to have high aspirations and to expect more than perhaps parents expect of their children in the other schools [in areas of low deprivation]. It gets harder, in many respects, as they get older: adolescence cuts in and the context probably draws them back into it. It's a default mechanism, isn't it?" (Governor and local group member, interview, May 2014)

Some governors tried to make sense of the considerable difficulties encountered when trying to recruit new governors – in their view, it was partly down to negative media coverage of the role and the amount of work involved within it:

> "I don't know whether it is partly the media information with parent governors, and the expectations and concerns, but certainly I feel that they think it is maybe about them and they can't cope with it – which is a shame." (Governor trustee and local group member, interview, April 2014)

The following governor stressed that, like anything, an insider's view of the role was different to an outsider's view:

> "There are these perceptions, you know, but we have also got a responsibility to reassure people that it's not that onerous because you can become involved with certain bits and you don't have to be involved in the peripheral bits, and all of these instructions and rules that come out." (Governor, interview, April 2014)

The following governor felt that governors were often held up by parents as "the fount of all knowledge" in education matters, whereas, in reality, it was the very fact that governors knew little about education that enabled them to challenge more effectively: "It doesn't matter if you ask a silly question because, you know, it is much better that governors ask the basic questions and, you know, as school governors, we have to do something to allay the fears of people" (governor trustee and local group member, interview, May 2014).

A bridge between community and school

Making sense of the role in terms of asking the *naive questions* appeared to be a way of compensating for what a number of governors perceived to be their lack of knowledge about education and pedagogy. It also demonstrated that for many governors, the community was a very powerful reference group. For many governors in this study, this seemed to be a far stronger reference point, and a measure of how well the school was performing, than influence from the head and senior leadership team – a trait that has been criticised in a number of reports into school governance, particularly those emanating from the inspectorate (see, eg, Ofsted, 2002, 2004, 2011a).

A number of governors made sense of their role by thinking of it in terms of a bridge between the school and community, as the following governor explained:

"There is a culture that pulls them [the students] back and the relationship between school and parents is quite difficult based on their own history. And it's about breaking down that barrier as well, and so I think that governors have a big part to play with that. I think they do in terms of sharing the message and spreading the word." (Governor and local group member, interview, May 2014)

Some governors indicated that the task was constant – that "there should be no let-up" (governor in federation 2, interview, May 2014). They made sense of their work in the context of combat, of a fight that was and always would be (in their opinion) one against the lack of student aspiration:

"I know there is social deprivation in the area – I live in the area, I know the area – but there are enterprising people around, even in a deprived area. And whilst there are problems, students coming from a second generation where their parents may not have had a regular job on a long-term basis, and it does play its part, there are a lot of youngsters who are striving to have their own dreams, ambitions and aspirations. And I think our role as governors is to make sure that the school has the support it needs to develop those aspirations and drive them." (Governor trustee and local group member, interview, May 2014)

Governors interviewed for this project all saw their work as firmly rooted in the community – their concerns were for the community and went much wider than the school, as the following governor describes:

"For me it's about getting what is best for X town, not just for our students, but about getting what is right for students and young people in the whole of this town. I know we are talking about X school on one side of the town and Y school – a different type of school – on the other, but it is really important that, collectively, we all try to do the best for the young people in the area, regardless of what type of school it is." (Governor and local group member, interview, April 2014)

Making sense of their role and decisions, using the community as a reference point, offered a helpful breadth of purpose in terms of both school strategy and the curriculum. Schools viewed in this way were central to influencing how communities were formed and shaped.

Challenge and support, but who?

Challenge and support has been a mantra for the inspectorate in terms of governance for some time now (Ofsted, 2002, 2004, 2008, 2014, 2015a, 2015b). Challenging the senior leadership team has traditionally been seen as a difficult area for all governing bodies but particularly testing for those in areas of deprivation (Deem et al, 1995; James et al, 2011). Placing this challenge in terms of the school context was, according to the following governor, relatively easy if the focus was on elements that influenced student performance:

"I think governors should be challenging the leadership around the things that are indicators of the areas in which you work, so, for example, we should be challenging around what the head is doing to get the children into school. We know what they are doing to support so we should be focusing on these as indicators and challenging around that." (Governor and local group member, interview, April 2014)

Governors did appear to be trying to make sense of how far this challenge should go and when it was appropriate to challenge and support. At times, they seemed to struggle and several commented that it was an area where they felt that they needed some examples from other governing bodies:

"I think the governing body is about supporting the school with a set of skills, yes, but the real skill you bring is to constructively challenge and hold the head to account, and occasionally, if there is a really difficult situation ... then it is absolutely the right thing to do – to support them – but actually also doing work to change the outcomes of the school. I'm really not sure whether this is the correct thing to do but it would be interesting to see whether other governing bodies have felt the same." (Governor and local group member, interview, April 2014)

The colaborated structures of the schools were seen to be quite helpful in combating this sense of isolation, with governors often having roles on local groups (assigned to single schools with no decision-making powers), as well as being part of the main governing body or trust directors. This was in contrast to those with a single role, who often felt more disconnected from individual schools within the trust, as the following governor reported: "It's not quite the same – I don't feel so on top of local issues" (trust director, interview, April 2014).

Growing the vision: growing into the vision

For governors in this project, the whole area around strategy appeared to be focused around the growth of the trust. However, this was seen as a challenging area: some governors regularly slipped into talking about 'the school' rather than 'the group of schools', suggesting that the understandings of strategy and vision that had been gained in the course of work with a single school were difficult to adapt to the trust as a whole. In addition to this, there were strong indications that forming a definite strategy for a whole group of schools was a difficult area for governors and one in which justifications attached to meanings and interpretations lacked conviction and, in many cases, commitment to a course of action to expand the group. This is perhaps unsurprising given the dearth of information on scaling up school structures, a trend reflected in a more mature body of research into the growth of charter management organisations in the US. This research reflects the considerable challenges encountered when scaling up these organisations (see, eg, Wohlstetter et al, 1994; Farrell et al, 2012).

Making sense of overall strategy appeared to involve a complex amalgam of community and school-based factors that proved difficult to bring together. Decisions were often self-referenced: governors looked to what they had decided as a body in the past and looked back to earlier understandings around values, ethos and strategic aims for one or two schools in the group, then made attempts to use this as a springboard for thinking about future strategy, as the following governor trustee reported:

> Ok, they have taken on board X school and that is all fine, but it's what the vision is: how we want it to grow [is the issue], so we put some caveats in around that and talk about things such as what is going to be of value to the organisation and how it [expansion] is going to benefit the children. It was trying to provide some parameters in which decisions could be made and the expansion – that was the one we were really thinking about because we haven't covered that – but were also looking at previous statements we'd made about what we wanted the school to be and what we wanted it to look like." (Governor trustee and local group member, interview, April 2014)

Part of the struggle in setting a strategic direction for the group seemed to go hand in hand with difficulties in accepting new understandings of their role. These meanings often sat uncomfortably with old, 'established' ways of looking at things. Professional skills came to the fore in this instance and were employed as a reference point to make sense of areas that were proving difficult. In the following example, monitoring non-financial performance was initially seen to be very challenging by the governor until they framed it within the context of their business background:

> "It's very difficult as a non-educationalist to say 'Well, I don't think that approach will work but if you try that one it will'. What you are looking at is the thought and preparation that goes into whatever plans the head has produced – you have

confidence that those plans will be followed – you have to rely on the principal to really endorse those plans. When the attainment data is presented in a way which businesspeople like myself can understand – like payment and profit compared to previous periods, so we can compare it to what might be expected – then you can do a bit of your own research and see how it compares to other schools." (Governor trustee, interview, May 2014)

Distance from individual schools was, as mentioned earlier, problematic for some governors; however, some trust directors felt that it was this very distance that enabled them to take the more strategic overview that is a key element within the governor role – even if it felt uncomfortable. The following governor reflects on how – even though they are aware of the fact that the inevitable distance between them and the individual schools in the trust may well be healthy in terms of strategic overview – it feels very much as if they are out of their comfort zone precisely because their knowledge of detail is necessarily far less than they were used to when governing a single school:

"The upside is that you can be extremely clear thinking and you are not caught up in the detail of it and so you can be very, very challenging, which is often why companies very successfully use non-executive directors, so I can see that. But my personal preference is very much more for knowing the nuts and bolts than we can ever know in the director role." (Director and local group governor, interview, March 2014)

While acknowledging that a business background could be useful in governing, some governors also felt that it had a downside: "They [governors from a business background] see things in very simple terms, but children aren't like commodities – and success is tricky to measure, if you measure it right" (governor trustee, interview, May 2014).

Working with the head teacher – a vital part of strategy – was felt to be a tricky area, particularly in the sense of retaining a professional distance and objective approach when governors were confident that the head was effective:

> "I think that the biggest risk, and this is not necessarily for the whole organisation, but I feel this with both the governing bodies that I sit on, is that they have both got quite an inspirational head. I feel there is a big risk that all they want to do is support that type of head and be their friend, and, you know, give them every support they can. I think that the biggest risk is then that you don't spot issues because you'll be too focused on showing the head teacher as being firm [and talented]. And, of course, that's important – it's a really lonely job – but I think it can go too far and it can stop being appropriately challenging while it can become a bit of a back-slapping situation and I thought that with X school [which dropped to inadequate rating from good in recent inspection]." (Governor and local group member, interview, April 2014)

The following governor also felt that they had been sucked into too great a reliance on the head, and it came of something of a shock when Ofsted downgraded the school: "I felt that the meetings were extremely positive and X is without a doubt an extremely capable leader, then, all of a sudden, the Ofsted report comes through and I don't think any of us were really expecting it" (governor and local group member, interview, May 2014).

Making sense of having had great faith in a leader and subsequently being faced with the school's demise in terms of the Ofsted judgement came through as a very difficult area in terms of sense-making. It challenged governors' confidence in their own judgement and, in some cases, shook the foundations of their understanding of the role. In the case of the following governor, they had previously made sense of their role in terms of the relationship between the governing body and senior leadership team, a partnership that they previously believed to be a strength. The negative Ofsted rating made them question their positive understandings of their own and the senior leadership team's work as they were forced to confront the fact that further down the hierarchy, things just were not working as they should have been:

> "Why would those two heads of department be allowed to decide not to implement what was clearly a very good system? I mean, there might be a good reason but an unacceptable reason would be, well, they didn't feel like it and we never got around to persuading them why that would be a good idea … and we [governors] need to know why that was." (Governor trustee, interview, April 2014)

This sense of being let down by the senior leadership was combined with a frustration that it would not have happened had they, the governors, been in the head teacher's shoes and been more operationally involved in implementing strategies. Although there was no sense that they could have done anything about this, their failure to monitor these evident flaws in the system proved frustrating for them – not only frustrating, but also difficult to come to terms with in regards to their own role. It was easy to make sense of the situation – the head had not implemented the strategy successfully – but not so easy to know how they, the governors, could have been expected to be aware of that, or, indeed, how they would remedy the situation in the future.

Roles and contributions: old understandings, new framework?

Governing, as the earlier chapters described, is a complex, time-consuming and sometimes thankless task, but this study reported that while governors felt challenged by new structures and ways of operating, they all had faith that governing a group of schools in areas of high socio-economic deprivation was potentially far more effective in terms of the advantages that it brought to pupils and communities. While the work was often hard – described as a "struggle" or "fight" – their motivation to continue performing the role, in most cases, came from a deep sense of purpose that what they were doing was not only aiding students and schools, but also helping to transform communities marred by high unemployment and the effects of economic austerity. While governors were getting to grips with new, sometimes hierarchical, governing structures, these very structures were also presenting them with challenges that weighed heavily on top of an already difficult job.

One of the key challenges within the role appeared to be keeping up with the numerous changes in school legislation and regulation and ensuring that these changes were communicated to the group as a whole. However, by far the most significant challenge in terms of sense-making was that of ensuring that the school had a firm strategic focus. Confidence in this area was largely lacking and apparently absent from any training and development offered locally. This small study would tend to suggest that this should be the focus of a more extensive study in the future.

Note

[1]. There is no overarching evidence base for this as, at the time of writing, no national records are kept of either who governors are or how long they remain in post.

SEVEN

POST-TROJAN HORSE: CHANGES TO POLICY AND PRACTICE SINCE THE TROJAN HORSE AFFAIR

Introduction

This book set out to examine how political and cultural changes have affected the governance of English schools and how one particular episode, the Trojan Horse affair, brought to light the many issues created largely due to intense and rapid changes within the structure of English education. Chapter Six focused on some of the challenges that governors are facing in making sense of their complex working environment. In this final chapter, I examine how the Trojan Horse affair became a catalyst for even greater and more sweeping changes to governing policy and practices, and discuss the implications of these for school governing.

Political fallout

The Trojan Horse affair began in March 2014 and the investigations into it by the Office for Standards in Education, Children's Services and Skills (Ofsted), the Department for Education (DfE), the Education Funding Agency and Birmingham City Council (BCC) were concluded by July the same year. As Chapter Two described, the outcomes of the reports indicated that while there was little evidence to support allegations of an extremist plot, there was evidence that there had been considerable failures in governance and that local oversight of schools in the current system had been considerably compromised by cuts to funding within BCC, along with sweeping changes to education. As also explained earlier, the Kershaw report (undertaken on behalf of the BCC) indicated that cuts imposed on BCC over the course of the previous five years seriously impacted on school support and overview, with staff numbers in this area being reduced from 170 to just 20. This led the report to conclude that 'BCC does not possess the capacity to robustly undertake investigations into complaints about governance or leadership in schools' (Kershaw, 2014, p 5).

The political fallout from the affair was spectacular. Education Secretary Michael Gove's involvement came to a head in early June 2014, when a row between him and Home Secretary Theresa May hit the headlines. The row was apparently provoked by public statements from the Education Secretary to the effect that the Home Office had 'failed to drain the swamp of radicalised Islam in the UK' and that it was this that had led to the debacle. This was followed by a letter, written and allegedly leaked by Theresa May, in which the Home Secretary appeared to accuse Gove of having failed to act on information that had been received by the DfE as long ago as 2010, and that BCC was warned about the alleged plot even earlier, in 2008. This was later backed up in the press when *The Guardian* interviewed Tim Boyes, head of a Birmingham school, who publicly stated that he had met with a minister and officials twice in 2010 to discuss Muslim hard-liners infiltrating schools but that no action was taken (*The Guardian*, 2014). The row escalated to such an extent that Prime Minister David Cameron was forced to intervene in order to restore calm, a move that was attributed by the media to the imminence of the Queen's Speech some days later.

On 14 June 2014, David Cameron removed Michael Gove from his position as Education Secretary, a move that was roundly criticised in the right-wing press. An article in *The Spectator*, published in July 2014 just after the Clarke report, criticised David Cameron for demoting Gove, declaring that the publication of the Clarke report 'vindicated' Gove's decision to appoint the ex-anti-terrorist chief, stating that:

> The Trojan Horse affair is exactly about subversion. As with the original beast, our own guards failed to spot what was within the gates. When Margaret Thatcher was education secretary in the early 1970s, the Chief Rabbi, Immanuel Jakobovits, told her that her job made her 'the real minister of defence in this country'. Islamists understand that concept, and work ceaselessly to weaken that defence. Mr Cameron has moved the only minister who really understood this. As Prime Minister, he directs the security agencies. If he is proud of the Gove legacy, as he says he is, he should charge them to investigate subversion once more. (Moore, 2014)

In Gove's place, David Cameron appointed Nicky Morgan, Conservative MP for Loughbrough, in a move that was publicly framed as an attempt to 'increase higher numbers of female representatives in senior cabinet positions' (Mason, 2014).

Whatever the motivation for the move, in a speech on 22 July 2014, Nicky Morgan set out her position on the Trojan Horse affair and what she termed 'fundamental British values':

> Advice to the panel already provides that actions which undermine fundamental British values should be viewed as misconduct. I will strengthen that advice to make clear that exposing pupils to extremist speakers should be regarded as a failure to protect pupils and promote British values. I will also strengthen the advice to make it clear that prohibition from teaching should be imposed while such cases are investigated and a prohibition without review made where misconduct is proved. (Morgan, 2014)

This was not the first time that the term 'British values' had entered the lexicon of government, as Robin Richardson points out:

'The British', wrote the editors of *Political Quarterly* in 2000, introducing a special issue on national identity to mark the arrival of the new millennium, 'have long been distinguished by having no clear idea about who they are, where they are, or what they are. Most of them have routinely described England as Britain. Only business people talk about a place called the United Kingdom.... It is all a terrible muddle' (Gamble and Wright, 2000, p 1). A few years later a character in a feature film set in Glasgow happened to introduce herself in these terms: 'I am a Glaswegian Pakistani teenage woman of Muslim descent who supports Glasgow Rangers in a Catholic school ... I'm a mixture and I'm proud of it [*Ae Fond Kiss*, also known as *Just a Kiss*, directed by Ken Loach, 2004]. (Richardson, 2015)

However, debates around what it means to be 'British' had intensified against a background of national unrest. The Parekh (2000) report, produced by the Commission on the Future of Multi-Ethnic Britain for the Runnymede Trust in 2000, attributed this to four principal factors:

- globalisation in its various dimensions and the consequent decline in the power and legitimacy of national governments;
- increasing pluralism in personal moral values and lifestyles, particularly in relation to sexual relations and family and household structures, and associated declines in deference and trust for tradition;
- the decline of manufacturing and mining industries and, in consequence, of hitherto secure employment prospects for a large proportion of the population; and
- the decline in the prestige of Christianity combined with the realities and associated anxieties of post-imperialism.

In terms of education policy, the whole issue of what constitutes a 'British value' had been raised some years earlier in discussions around 'character education'. James Arthur (2005, p 240), writing in the journal *Educational Studies*, had asked whether 'it is possible in a heterogeneous society, composed of people who disagree sharply about basic values, to achieve a consensus about what constitutes character education for citizens in a democracy'.

Despite this, however, the government had already published a consultation on strengthening independent school standards, which also applied to academies and free schools, which included the 'requirement to actively promote British Values' (DfE, 2014c). Added to this, Morgan's speech also set out her intention for Ofsted to 'inspect how well all schools are actively promoting fundamental British Values through their curriculum' and to 'bar unsuitable persons from running independent schools, including academies and free schools. Anyone barred in this way will also be prohibited from being a governor in any maintained school' (Morgan, 2014).

The Coalition government's use of the term 'British values' originally emanated from a Home Office document, which stated:

> Extremism is vocal or active opposition to fundamental British values, including democracy, the rule of law, individual liberty and mutual respect and tolerance of different faiths and beliefs. We also include in our definition of extremism calls for the death of members of our armed forces, whether in this country or overseas. (HM Government, 2011, p 107, cited in Richardson, 2015, p 41)

'British values' and the policing of 'British values'

Section 1 of the Education Reform Act 1988 already imposes a duty for all state-controlled schools to promote the '"Spiritual, moral, cultural, mental and physical development of pupils at the school and of society" and to prepare pupils "for the opportunities, responsibilities and experiences of adult life"', and the mention of specifically British values provoked an outcry on social media from teachers who demanded, among other things, why government obsession with values should declare them 'specifically British'. There was also a great deal of concern about how this policy would be 'policed' by the inspectorate, schools and governors (for more detail on the issues, see Rustin, 2015; Weale, 2015).

Ofsted did not emerge from the Trojan Horse affair unscathed, as a later inquiry into the affair by the House of Commons Education Committee would report (Gov.uk, 2015). Media coverage of inspections had been almost wholly negative and Muslim communities in Birmingham (and the rest of the country) and the public were confused by the fact that in a number of cases, the schools concerned had previously received very positive inspections; for example, Oldknow Academy was subject to a full inspection in January 2013 and was judged to be 'outstanding' in all categories. Its inspection post-Trojan Horse resulted in a downgrade to 'special measures' (the lowest Ofsted category). This raised some serious doubts about the consistency and fairness of the inspection process (and, indeed, the inspectors themselves).

Previous public statements by Sir Michael Wilshaw, particularly in relation to Park View School – the school at the centre of the row – in which he had lauded schools for outstanding performance, served to compound public feelings that the inspectorate was neither consistent nor reliable in its judgements (see Adams, 2014). Many from the world of education were also unhappy about the way in which Ofsted had carried out the inspections. In a letter to *The Guardian* signed by a number of education experts, Sir Tim Brighouse – former Chief Education Officer in Birmingham – stated that:

> First-hand accounts of the Ofsted inspections that have emerged are disturbing. They suggest that inspectors were poorly prepared and had an agenda that calls into question Ofsted's claim to be objective and professional in its appraisal of standards in schools serving predominantly Muslim pupils.
>
> Numerous sensationalised leaks have reinforced public perception of a pre-set government agenda. In a letter to *The Guardian* on the 3rd June 2014, a number of Educationalists, race

relations experts, human rights and community representatives expressed their dismay at what they saw as a debacle stating:

> It is beyond belief that schools which were judged less than a year ago to be 'outstanding' are now widely reported as 'inadequate', despite having the same curriculum, the same students, the same leadership team and the same governing body. In at least one instance, these conflicting judgments were made by the same lead inspector. This has damaged not only the reputation of the schools but the integrity of the inspections process. (Brighouse et al, letter to *The Guardian*, 3rd June 2014)

> This is uncharted territory, with Ofsted seemingly being guided by an ideology at odds with the traditional British values which schools are meant to espouse, particularly fairness, justice and respect for others. We, the undersigned, believe that such an approach compromises not only Ofsted's impartiality but also the British education system itself. (Brighouse, 2014)

The Clarke report also criticised the inspectorate, stating: 'Ofsted should consider whether the existing framework and associated guidance is capable of detecting indicators of extremism and ensuring that the character of a school is not changed substantively without following proper process' (Clarke, 2014, p 38).

In terms of school governance, the key message to emerge from reports by Ofsted, Kershaw and Clarke was clear – school governance had been at fault. The Trojan Horse Review Group (2014) (see Box 7.1) summed up the issues in a single statement: 'The central challenge emerging from [Kershaw's] investigation and related matters is the credibility and transparency of the framework within which school governors operate'.

Box 7.1: The Trojan Horse Review Group

Members
Amra Bone: Birmingham Central Mosque
Liam Byrne MP: Member of Parliament, Hodge Hill
Assistant Chief Constable (ACC) Garry Forsyth: West Midlands Police
Kamal Hanif: Headteacher Waverley School
Peter Hay: Strategic Director, BCC
Councillor Zafar Iqbal: BCC
Councillor Brigid Jones: Cabinet Member, BCC
Emma Knight: National Governors' Association (NGA)
Andrew Mitchell MP: Member of Parliament, Sutton Coldfield
Councillor James McKay: Cabinet Member, BCC
Christine Mitchell: Headteacher Clifton Primary
Stephen Rimmer: Chair of Review Group, West Midlands Strategic
Leader Preventing Violence to Vunerable People
Councillor Habib Rehman: BCC
Fran Stevens: Birmingham Governors' Network
Bishop David Urquhart: Bishop of Birmingham

Participant observer
Paul Rowsell: Department for Communities and Local Government

Emma Knights, speaking on behalf of the NGA following the release of the Clarke and Kershaw reports, emphasised that it was only a small group of governors in a system that numbered thousands, but that the problems highlighted by the affair did need to be addressed with some urgency:

It is of course of great concern that small groups of activists attempted to use the role of school governor or academy trustee to subvert the ethos of some schools in east Birmingham to emphasise the differences between cultures, rather than fostering tolerance and equality. We acknowledge that all the inspections and investigations into the Trojan Horse allegations found examples of poor governance; and much work needs to be done to ensure that governance is of a high standard in every school in England. The reports also raise bigger questions which remain to be answered in detail, such as how schools, including academies, are overseen (between inspections) and the role of faith and worship within our schools. (Knights, 2014)

The statement by Knights sums up some of the challenges for schools and their governance, a triad that includes: a dearth of local oversight; the complexity of oversight in terms of curricular provision; and the challenges of oversight and governance within an increasingly complex system.

The Trojan Horse affair – crafted by the media and manipulated by the government – has had substantial impact on education policy. The event was followed up by a number of similar incidents in which schools in Luton and Tower Hamlets were investigated for the same type of 'takeover plots' as the earlier event in Birmingham. These were also characterised by intense media attention, as I reported in an article for *The Conversation* in December 2014:

The results of seven school inspections in the London Borough of Tower Hamlets have brought a fresh wave of allegations that some schools are not providing a broad and balanced curriculum for their pupils, who may be vulnerable to radicalisation. A memorandum on the inspections sent by Ofsted's chief inspector of schools Michael Wilshaw to the education secretary Nicky Morgan has upped the ante in debates that conflate conservative religious values with the risk of radicalisation and extremism.

In six independent schools that were visited in the borough, inspectors found serious concerns over the safeguarding and welfare of pupils, lack of provision of a broad and balanced curriculum and issues around leadership, management and teaching.

Four of the six independent Muslim schools have been judged inadequate, with two failing to meet independent school standards. The only maintained school involved in the recent inspections, Sir John Cass in Stepney, was also downgraded by Ofsted from outstanding to inadequate. This followed concerns about segregation between boys and girls in school areas and insufficient guidance on 'the dangers associated with using the internet, particularly in relation to extremist views'. (Baxter, 2014)

Policy changes

The impact of these high-profile investigations on the communities in which they were situated has had a ripple effect, colouring the relationship between Muslim communities and the British state. Relationships built up over years were compromised by suspicion and doubt as schools that had previously been lionised were downgraded.

Both the original Trojan Horse affair and subsequent investigations in other schools driven by media attention and intense government interest became the catalysts for an intense wave of policy change. In the concluding part of this chapter, I explore what those changes have been and their implications for school governing from 2015 onwards.

Within weeks of an election in which a fully Conservative government under David Cameron was voted in, Education Secretary Nicky Morgan, continuing in her post, declared that the 'programme of reforms' set in motion during the previous administration would continue. Now unmediated by their Liberal Democrat coalition partners, the government pressed ahead with policies that would consolidate their position on the policing of 'British values' in the curriculum, alongside a drive to 'improve' schools via their continuing programme of academisation.

Government reaction to the Trojan Horse affair was, at the time, coloured and conditioned by Michael Gove's ideological stance, his 'paranoia' over the rise of Islamism combined with a strong sense that neither government nor security services were acting fast enough or effectively enough to prevent radicalisation taking hold of British schools and communities. However, changes in public opinion on radicalisation were also influenced by broader issues around extremism.

During the period immediately following the Trojan Horse affair, the British press also became sensitised to a new phenomenon: the rise of ISIS, or Islamic State.[1] The 'Islamic State', an extremist group that rose to world prominence in 2014, was created in 2006 following the death of Abu Musab al-Zarqawi, a Jordanian who had originally pledged alliance to Osama bin Laden and set up al-Quaeda in Iraq. The group began to hit national headlines in June 2014 when it overran the northern city of Mosul, and moving south towards the town of Baghdad, massacred all who stood in its path. At the end of June, the organisation declared that it had founded a caliphate and changed its name from ISIS to Islamic State in Iraq and Syria (Feldman, 2012; Hiro, 2013).

On 29 September 2014, *The Guardian* ran a report with the title: 'Schoolgirl jihadis: the female Islamists leaving home to join Isis fighters'. The report, written by a group of international journalists, drawing on work from the International Centre for the Study of Radicalisation (2015) and interviews from various Muslim associations, described the growing trend of radicalisation among schoolgirls as young as 13 (Sherwood et al, 2014).

On 22 February 2015, when three girls from Bethnal Green left their families and school to join the Islamic State, the whole issue of radicalisation in schools began to feel a lot 'closer to home'. The Prevent Strategy had been in place in schools for some time; originally part of the 2010–2015 Coalition government's counterterrorism strategy, it was aimed at preventing people 'becoming terrorists or supporting terrorism' (Gov.uk, 2011). The original document states that it fulfils this aim by means of a variety of strategies:

The Prevent Strategy:

- responds to the ideological challenge we face from terrorism and aspects of extremism, and the threat we face from those who promote these views
- provides practical help to prevent people from being drawn into terrorism and ensure they are given appropriate advice and support

- works with a wide range of sectors (including education, criminal justice, faith, charities, online and health) where there are risks of radicalisation that we need to deal with
- the strategy covers all forms of terrorism, including far right extremism and some aspects of non-violent extremism. However, we prioritise our work according to the risks we face. (Gov.uk, 2011)

The Clarke report specifically linked the failings of the schools in the Trojan Horse affair to a 'vulnerability to radicalisation'; it also pointed to the 'benign neglect' shown by the DfE and Ofsted when the schools' results and financial performance gave no cause for concern. As far as governors were concerned, Clarke reported that:

At Park View and other schools, governors have overstepped their responsibilities by restricting schemes of work and insisting on an Islamic approach to subjects, such as PSHE [personal, social and health education], science, religious education, and sex and relationships education.

Governors in several schools pay lip service to the Prevent Strategy, while continuing to restrict topics, such as forced marriage and female genital mutilation. (Clarke, 2014)

The events that began with the Trojan Horse affair were compounded by wider issues around terrorism and extremism, and in the face of growing public concern, the government responded in the creation of a new Act: the Counter-Terrorism and Security Act 2015. This Act places a statutory duty on organisations – including schools – to report individuals suspected of being 'at risk of radicalisation'. The links between terrorism and extremism presuppose that there is a direct link between conservative religious views and radicalisation, leading concomitantly to terrorist activity. The legislation places an enormous burden on schools and governors to pinpoint pupils they believe to be at risk of radicalisation and to take the appropriate action.

This move was combined with a mandate for all state schools to instil 'British values' in pupils.

The new emphasis on British values appears throughout the inspection regime, revised in 2015 following the Trojan Horse affair. Within the new regime, inspectors will judge how successfully the school (and, more specifically, the leadership of the school, including governors) carry out the following:

- provide learning programmes or a curriculum that have suitable breadth, depth and relevance so that they meet any relevant statutory requirements, as well as the needs and interests of children, learners and employers, nationally and in the local community
- successfully plan and manage learning programmes, the curriculum and careers advice so that all children and learners get a good start and are well prepared for the next stage in their education, training or employment
- actively promote equality and diversity, tackle bullying and discrimination and narrow any gaps in achievement between different groups of children and learners
- actively promote British values [see Gov.uk, 2011]
- make sure that safeguarding arrangements to protect children, young people and learners meet all statutory and other government requirements, promote their welfare and prevent radicalisation and extremism. (Ofsted, 2015b, s 28)

According to Ofsted (2015), 'fundamental British values' are:

- democracy;
- the rule of law;
- individual liberty and mutual respect; and
- tolerance of those with different faiths and beliefs.

Speaking on LBC radio on 16 June 2015, Sir Michael Wilshaw confirmed that the new framework would look to fail schools that did not actively promote British values, once again conflating the discourses of extremism, terrorism and conservative religious views:

> Schools must teach children 'British values' to fight the pull of jihadist groups....
>
> The teaching of British values is central to stopping youngsters joining the terror gang.... It is worrying and it is shocking. We are inspecting against British values at the moment. And when this was introduced by the government, people said to me 'Is this an extra burden on Ofsted and your HMI Inspectors.' And I said 'no, it's one of the most important things that we do.'
>
> It's really important that all schools, be they faith or non-faith schools, whether in mono-cultural communities or not, teach British values – the importance of tolerance and understanding other cultures and faiths. And if they don't do that, if they don't promote tolerance, then we will mark them down and we will fail them as we have done in some cases. You can tell very quickly whether a school is doing that or not and if they're not doing that, they are going to fail their Ofsted inspection. (Ferrari, 2015)

Within a single speech, he brought together elements that had been 'drip-fed' to the public in a discourse that the government and media had been crafting since the Trojan Horse affair: school failure; lack of adherence to 'British values'; and extremism. In a single utterance, he cut through the numerous cross-party protests about defining these values as specifically British, and paved the way for schools to be taken over or academised at the discretion of the inspectorate. The speech also paved the way for a government call for 'character education' based on 'British values' that would 'prepare' students for 'life in modern Britain'.

The narrative that conflates extremist speech and beliefs with terrorism has been contested by many researchers working in the field of counterterrorism. David Cameron, speaking at the Munich Security Conference in 2011, stated that:

Islam is a religion, observed peacefully and devoutly by over a billion people. Islamist extremism is a political ideology, supported by a minority. Time and again, people equate the two. They think whether someone is an extremist is dependent on how much they observe their religion.

So they talk about 'moderate' Muslims as if all devout Muslims must be extremist. This is wrong.

Someone can be a devout Muslim and not be an extremist.

We need to be clear: Islamist extremism and Islam are not the same thing. (Cameron, 2011)

However, while appearing to speak out against conflating the two, he then went on to criticise what he termed to be the 'doctrine of state multiculturalism', describing how, in his view, '*when equally unacceptable views or practices have come from someone who isn't white, we've been too cautious, frankly even fearful, to stand up to them*'.

Sociologist Oliver Roy, in his analysis of two main approaches to studying the roots of radicalisation in a paper for the Institute of Development at the University of Sussex, Brighton, suggests that 'The success of Osama Bin Laden is not to have established a modern and efficient Islamist political organisation, but to have invented a narrative that could allow rebels without a cause to connect with a cause' (Roy, 2008, p 5). He also argues that 'Ideology plays little role in the radicalisation of the jihadist internationalist youth: they are attracted by a narrative not an ideology' (Roy, 2008, p 8).

Although there is little scope to explore such a clearly complex area within a book such as this, it is clear that the whole area around values education is a complex one. Conservative governments have a long history of placing an emphasis on character education and the values that align with it. What has never been agreed upon are the values that are integral to producing an individual of 'good character'. In 1996, the Conservative government under John Major established a 'National Forum for Values in Education and the Community, which sought to discover whether there were any values on which there was 'common agreement in society' (Arthur, 2005, p 242). The forum, which then continued under Labour, produced a set of 'consensus ideals' agreed by 95% of respondents to a poll of 1,500 adults (Arthur, 2005, p 243). An extensive review of learning and teaching about values, carried out by Mark Halstead and Monica Taylor on behalf of the University of Plymouth and the National Foundation for Educational Research (NFER), analysed the whole area of values teaching and concluded that there was a need for schools to have a coherent strategy for values education, but that understanding of values development and methods of values education should be built into the initial and in-service training of teachers (Halstead and Taylor, 2000).

However, the idea of specifically 'British values' has caused a great deal of consternation for all faith schools, not just the purely Muslim variety. Trevor Cooling, Professor of Christian Education, writing in *The Times Educational Supplement*, outlines some of his concerns:

> However, in the current climate in which visceral fear about extremism is combined with secularist angst about religion, the danger is that people of more conservative religious faith become the ones that society thinks should 'clear off' out of education because they take their religion just a bit too seriously for British comfort. (Cooling, 2014)

He goes on to describe how the introduction of a similar policy in Australia resulted in a number of 'unintended consequences' when a poster advertising these values illustrated that they were aimed at a 'very particular type of Australian' – white, male and European (Cooling, 2014).

There are also considerable concerns about the effects of shutting down dialogue with pupils about the meaning of radicalisation and Islamism. New anti-radicalisation software being developed in response to the Counter-Terrorism and Security Act 2015 is being 'bought up like hot cakes' by schools. According to a spokeswoman for one of the organisations developing the software, it is designed to:

Help teachers confirm identification of vulnerable children, or act as an early warning system to help identify children that may be at risk in future. It also provides evidence for teachers and child protection officers to use in order to intervene and support a child in a timely and appropriate manner.

It is not about criminalising children, it is about helping schools spot the early warning signs so that risk in relation to an individual can be assessed and measured, and counter-narratives and support can be put in place to help educate children before they potentially become victims of radicalisation. (Taylor, 2015)

However, there is considerable concern that this type of intervention will stigmatise students and prevent the type of open discussion that is precisely what is needed to open up dialogue and prevent radicalisation. Farid Panjwani, writing about the teaching of Islam in secular schools, believes that a rethink is needed on the whole way that the Islamic curriculum is taught in schools, and that it needs 'significant changes' in the wake of the Trojan Horse affair. She is particularly concerned with what she terms the process of 'religiofication – a process of turning practical everyday matters into holy causes – 'the tendency in textbooks about Islam to define Muslim cultures primarily in religious terms' (Panjwani, 2014, p 10), feeling that this offers a less than balanced view of what being a Muslim should entail:

Surveying the syllabuses and textbooks on Islam one gets the impression that Islam dominates the lives of its followers, providing them with identities, practices, moral sense and values. Being a Muslim thus can only mean being a religious person whose entire life from rituals to politics is shaped by Islam. (Panjwani, 2014, p 9)

Panjwani believes that religiofication of Muslim communities functions as 'the perpetrator of an unhelpful alterity', and that the Trojan Horse affair may well have been a turning point in 'the better teaching of Muslim cultures in schools', something that would offer a deeper understanding of the 'complex intersection of the secular and the religious in public and private lives' (Panjwani, 2014, p10).

The outlook for school governing: 2015 onwards

The implications for school governing emanating from the political and educational fallout from the Trojan Horse affair have, as this chapter has explained, been considerable. The new legislation that requires schools and governors to maintain a vigil against radicalisation is yet another burden on an already overloaded job specification. As Chapter Six reported, governors are still making sense of multi-level governance structures, new accountabilities and increased responsibilities. Studies in school governance have, as this book has explained, pointed up areas of difficulty that pose challenges for all boards in the not-for-profit sector, not just school governors.

While it is understandable that society should wish to make every effort to counter extremism in all its forms, for schools, there is a very fine line between detecting potential targets of radicalisation and stigmatising and criminalising schoolchildren. There is also a danger that the very measures used to track down and deal with extreme religious views will shut down the very debates that should be happening in schools. Unfortunately, this already appears to be happening, as an article in *The Guardian* (6 December 2015) illustrates:

> Muslim religious leaders in one of the most ethnically diverse boroughs in Britain have criticised the government's programmes to stop people turning to extremism and terrorist violence as 'divisive' and leading to a 'breakdown in trust'.
>
> In a rare sign of public discontent, east London imams – backed by teachers, community organisations and student unions – have claimed the measures adopted under The Anti Radicalisation Prevent Scheme and the Counter-Terrorism and Security Act result in 'spying on our young people' and lead to 'increasing division and to a breakdown of trust in schools and colleges'.

Governors, whose role is necessarily strategic rather than operational, will need to consider evidence presented to them very carefully when asked to become involved in these matters in their 'challenge and support' function.

In terms of the press, as Chapters Two and Three explained, it is very likely that now the media is sensitised to the whole area of governors and extremism, governors will come under increasing levels of media attention. Given the politicisation of school governing as a direct result of the affair, this reporting is very likely to appear in high-profile political sections of the news. The nature of this type of coverage renders governance a 'high-risk' activity for local people, many of whom have reputations tied into school outcomes. How events following the Trojan Horse affair are impacting on the recruitment of governors and teachers in affected schools is difficult to say; what is evident is that these issues are still causing concern for parents, teachers and governors. On 14 July 2015, an advice letter on school inspections in Birmingham and Tower Hamlets from Sir Michael Wilshaw was sent to the Secretary of State for Education. In it, he revealed concerns around the issue of children being removed from school, their destinations unknown, stating: 'We cannot be sure that some of the children whose destinations are unknown are not being exposed to harm, exploitation or the influence of extremist ideologies' (Wilshaw, 2015b). In addition to these new concerns (which solicited a policy response), he also reported that six of the 21 schools in Birmingham remain in special measures, 'mainly due to problems around stability of leadership and recruitment and retention of teaching staff' (Wilshaw, 2015b, p 2). A survey done in 2015 and completed by 1,320 governors reflected these recruitment issues, revealing that 48% of respondents found governor recruitment either fairly or very difficult (Key for School Governors, 2015).

The move to professionalise school governing detailed in Chapters Four and Five has created new challenges. Although governors may well come with a good set of professional skills, unless these are readily transferable to the education sector, they are less likely to translate into effective governance. Ensuring that governors receive the right sort of training that provides them with the skills to translate competencies and skills from other areas into the complex and demanding world of education may well demand a different approach to development than offerings that have evolved since the 1960s – an approach that focuses on some of the key elements of multi-level governance and takes an analytical view of strategy-setting in educational settings. As in any area, this will demand a realistic and fairly comprehensive knowledge of schools' operating context across all of the schools within a particular group, be they multi-academy trusts (MATs), chains or other forms of federation.

One policy response to a more cohesive approach to governor support has been the National Leaders of Governance (NLG) initiative, which began in 2012. The initiative, set up by the National College for Teaching and Leadership (NCTL), was designed to offer support from experienced chairs of governors to other chairs. Founded on a robust bank of evidence highlighting the primacy of the chair in forming and shaping effective governing bodies, the initiative was evaluated in 2014 by Ceri Matthias of BMG Research, acting for the NCTL (Matthias, 2014). Although the report was limited in scope – with perceptions of 267 deployments by NLG and only 79 evaluations completed by supported chairs and head teachers – the results appear to be fairly positive. However, guidance on the deployment of individuals is fairly vague and success would tend to depend on the extent to which chairs are responsive and act on recommendations, as well as on the skills of the particular adviser.

As Chapter Five outlined, there has been an exponential growth in focus on governor accountability, largely due to the changing structures within the education sector. These changes, combined with the demise of local education authorities (LEAs), have left a vacuum in terms of local accountability. In response to this, and following a report by the National Audit Office in October 2014, the DfE created eight new Regional School Commissioners (RSCs), accountable to a central School Commissioner. These commissioners are supported by head teacher boards. The powers of RSCs are devolved from the Secretary of State and include: authorising new academy conversions; issuing warning notices for failing academies; and making strategic decisions on the size and capacity of schools.

In 2015, the Queen's Speech suggested that RSCs will be given intervention powers in all schools – particularly those defined by Ofsted as 'coasting'. Unfortunately, their ability to act independently of government is highly suspect as they are targeted on the amount of schools they convert to academy status, as well as holding schools to account (Nye, 2015). Head teacher boards, composed of three different types of membership (see Box 7.2), may, by the very fact of their composition, be strongly focused on academies.

Box 7.2: Composition of elected head teacher boards

- Elected head teachers (all heads must come from an academy rated 'good' or 'outstanding' by Ofsted).
- Appointed members (chosen directly by the RSC – they do not have to be working in education).
- Co-opted (up to two members – normally based around a required skill set).

However, evidence being given to the Education Select Committee's inquiry into the role of RSCs suggests that governance is becoming increasingly complex and confusing, with an even wider range of actors involved in the whole area of accountability. As Ofsted's evidence to the committee suggests:

> The current overall level of engagement between RDs [regional representatives for Ofsted] and RSCs is variable. This is, in part, due to the different geographical areas covered by the established 'Ofsted regions' compared with the 'RSC regions'. As a result, some RDs have to engage with several RSCs. In contrast, other RDs have only had to develop links with one RSC. Nevertheless, all RDs are developing these relationships and already meet regularly with the RSCs overseeing academies and free schools in their region. (Ofsted, 2015c, RSC00041)

The Education Select Committee's final report into Regional Schools Commissioners was published on 20 January 2016 (Parliament, 2016). The Chair of the Committee, The Right Honourable Neil Carmichael, summed up the state of education governance as revealed by the evidence within the report, stating:

> For too long, and under all parties, the Department for Education has made changes to structures without setting out the big picture. Regional Schools Commissioners were introduced as a pragmatic response to a problem – the growing number of academies and the need for oversight of them. They're doing a necessary job, but the oversight system is now confused, fragmented, and lacking in transparency.
>
> It's hardly surprising that most people have never heard of RSCs, and even those who have are unclear about their role. RSCs are a product of the Department's 'acting first, thinking later' approach when it comes to big changes in the schools landscape. The DfE needs to take a long hard look at this picture once the number of academies stabilises, and design a more coherent system for the future which ensures proper accountability for schools.

School governing has come a long way in the past five years, from Chris James' 'hidden givers' – quietly working to support schools – to professionalised bodies and the subject of intense media and government scrutiny, with roles and responsibilities that rival the job descriptions of senior company directors. Yet, at the time of writing, they remain unpaid volunteers and, according to surveys carried out by the NGA, wish to remain so.

At a time when education in England is both fragmented and riddled with uncertainties, we can perhaps only be certain of one thing: that school governors remain central to a democratic system of school governance whatever shape and form it may take. The more we learn about these 'hidden givers', the better chance we have of supporting their valiant efforts to ensure that all children are offered a democratic education that maximises their potential and equips them with the skills to face the future – however uncertain that future may be.

Note

[1] See Introduction, note 2 for note on terminology.

References

Abbas, T. (2005) *Muslim Britain: Communities under pressure*, London: Zed Books.

Adam Smith Institute (1984) *Education policy: The Omega Report,* London: Adam Smith Institute.

Adams, R. (2014) 'Theresa May calls on Michael Gove to act on extremism in schools', *The Guardian*, 4 June. Available at: http://www.theguardian.com/politics/2014/jun/04/theresa-may-gove-extremism-schools-trojan-horse

Adams, R. (2015) 'Durham Free School to close, says education secretary', *The Guardian*, 25 February. Available at: http://www.theguardian.com/education/2015/feb/25/durham-free-school-to-close-education-secretary

Addley, E. (2012) 'Michael Gove gives Leveson inquiry a lesson in oration', *The Guardian*, 29 May. Available at: http://www.theguardian.com/media/2012/may/29/michael-gove-leveson-inquiry-sketch

Agyris, C. (1999) *On organisational learning*, Oxford: Blackwell.

Anderson, G.L. (2007) 'Media's impact on educational policies and practices: political spectacle and social control', *Peabody Journal of Education*, 82(1): 103–20.

Arthur, J. (2005) 'The re-emergence of character education in British education policy', *British Journal of Educational Studies*, 53(3): 239–54.

Audit Commission (1988a) *Surplus capacity in secondary schools: A progress report,* London: The Audit Commission.

Audit Commission (1988b) *Local Management of Schools: A note to Local Education Authorities,* London: The Audit Commission.

Audit Commission (1989) *Working for patients,* London: The Audit Commision

Audit Commission (1989) *Assuring quality in education: Report on local education authority inspectors and advisers*, London: The Audit Commission.

Avis, J. (1999) 'Shifting identity: new conditions and the transformation of practice – teaching within post-compulsory education', *Journal of Vocational Education & Training*, 51(2): 245–64.

Baker, K. (1986) *Turbulent years: My life in politics,* London: Faber.

Bagley, C., Woods, P. and Glatter, R. (1996) 'Scanning the market school strategies for discovering parental perspectives', *Educational Management Administration & Leadership*, 24(2): 125–38.

Bagley, C., Woods, P.A. and Glatter, R. (2001) 'Rejecting schools: towards a fuller understanding of the process of parental choice', *School Leadership & Management*, 21(3): 309–25.

Balarin, M., Brammer, S., James, C. and McCormack, M. (2008) *The school governance study*, Bath: The University of Bath.

Ball, S. (1993) 'Education markets, choice and social class: the market as a class strategy in the UK and the USA', *British Journal of Sociology of Education*, 14(1):3–19.

Ball, S. (2008) 'New philanthropy, new networks and new governance in education', *Political Studies*, 56(4): 747–65.

Ball, S. (2009) 'Academies in context: politics, business and philanthropy and heterarchical governance', *Management in Education*, 23(3): 100–3

Barber, M. (2009). 'From system effectivenes to system improvements: reform paradigms and relationships', in A. Hargreaves and M. Fullan (eds.), *Change wars*. Bloomington , IN: Solution Tree.

Barrett, D. (2010) '£300,000 bill for head teacher's uneaten cake; petty grievances at struggling grammar school led to bitter legal battle', *Sunday Telegraph*, 5 December, p 23.

Barthes, R. (2009) *Vintage Barthes* (trans A. Lavers), London: Vintage.

Bassey, A. (2014) 'Communities "have been damaged by Trojan Horse scandal"', *Birmingham Mail*, 27 July. Available at: http://www.birminghammail.co.uk/news/midlands-news/communities-damaged-trojan-horse-scandal-7512902

Baxter, J. (2011a) 'An investigation into the role of professional learning on the online teaching identities of higher education lecturers', unpublished EdD, The Open University.

REFERENCES

Baxter, J. (2011b) *Public centre professional identities: A review of the literature*, Milton Keynes: The Open University.

Baxter, J. (2011c) 'Public sector professional identities: evolution or etiolation? A review of the literature'. Available at: http://oro.open.ac.uk/29793/

Baxter, J. (2012) 'The impact of professional learning on the online teaching identities of higher education lecturers: the role of resistance discourse', *European Journal of Open, Distance and E-Learning*, 1(2). Available at: http://oro.open.ac.uk/34717/1/Baxter%20j%202012.pdf

Baxter, J. (2013) 'Professional inspector or inspecting professional? Teachers as inspectors in a new regulatory regime for education in England', *Cambridge Journal of Education*, 43(4): 467–85.

Baxter, J. (2014) 'Ofsted's future at stake after Trojan Horse Scandal, *The Conversation*, May 01. Available at :https://theconversation.com/ofsteds-future-at-stake-after-trojan-horse-scandal-25936

Baxter, J. (2014a) 'An independent inspectorate? Addressing the paradoxes of educational inspection in 2013', *School Leadership and Management*, 34(1). Available at: http://www.tandfonline.com/eprint/tY4sKEuNn6NBQAggrGkM/full

Baxter, J. (2014b) 'Policy briefing: Trojan Horse, the media and the Ofsted inspectorate', *Discover Society*, 1 July. Available at: http://www.discoversociety.org/2014/07/01/policy-briefing-trojan-horse-the-media-and-the-ofsted-inspectorate-2/

Baxter, J. (2014c) 'Naming, framing and shaming: the role and function of the media on education and inspection policy in England', European Educational Research Conference 'The Past, the Present and Future of Educational Research in Europe', Porto, Portugal, 1–5 September.

Baxter, J. (2015a) *Roles and identities of school governors study*, Milton Keynes: The Open University.

Baxter, J. (2015b) *Interim project report: Governors in the media*, Milton Keynes: The Open University.

Baxter, J. and Clarke, J. (2012) 'What counts as success in inspection in England – shifting criteria?', European Conference for Educational Research, Network 23 Symposium '"Governing by Inspection": National Developments', Cadiz, Spain, 18–21 September.

Baxter, J. and Clarke, J. (2013) 'Farewell to the tick box inspector? Ofsted and the changing regime of school inspection in England', *Oxford Review of Education*, 39(5): 702–18.

Baxter, J. and Farrell, C. (2015) 'Leadership and comparative models of governance in public services', Democracy, Inequality and Power: Redefining Classic Concepts Conference, Bristol, 15–16 September.

Baxter, J. and Rönnberg, L. (2014) 'Inspection and the media: the media and inspection', in S. Grek and J. Lindgren (eds) *Governing by inspection*, London: Routledge.

Baxter, J. and Wise, C. (2013) 'Federation governing: translation or transformation?', *Management in Education, Special Issue: Governing and Governance*, 27(3): 106–11.

BBC (2014) 'Trojan Horse probe headed by ex-Met chief Peter Clarke', *BBC News Regions: Birmingham and Black Country*, 15 April. Available at: http://www.bbc.co.uk/news/uk-england-birmingham-27031941

Beijaard, D., Meijer, P.C. and Verloop, N. (2004) 'Reconsidering research on teachers' professional identity', *Teaching and Teacher Education*, 20: 107–28.

Bennett, C. and Yanovitzky, I. (2000) 'Patterns of congressional news media use: the questions of selection bias and third person effect', paper presented at the American Political Sciences Association, Washington, DC.

Berliner, D. and Biddle, B. (1995) *The manufactured crisis: Myths, fraud, and the attack on America's public schools*, Cambridge, MA: Perseus Books.

Best, G., Dennis, J. and Draper, P. (1977) *Health, the mass media and the National Health Service*, London: Unit for the Study of Health Policy.

Beveridge, W. (1942) *Social insurance and allied services*, Cmd 6404 (Beveridge report), London: HM Stationery Office.

Bevir, M. (ed) (2013) *The Sage handbook of governance*, London: Sage.

Blackmore, J. and Thomson, P. (2004) 'Just "good and bad news"? Disciplinary imaginaries of head teachers in Australian and English print media', *Journal of Education Policy*, 19(3): 301–20.

Blyth, M. (2013) *Austerity: The history of a dangerous idea*, Oxford: Oxford University Press.

Boix, C. (1998) *Political parties, growth and equality: Conservative and social democratic economic strategies in the world economy*, Cambridge: Cambridge University Press.

REFERENCES

Bolsen, T. and Leeper, T.J. (2013) 'Self-interest and attention to news among issue publics', *Political Communication*, 30(3): 329–48.

Bowers, C.A. (2011) *Nick Clegg: The biography*, London: Biteback Publishing.

Boyne, G., Day, P. and Walker, R. (2002) 'The evaluation of public service inspection: a theoretical framework', *Urban Studies*, 39(7): 1197–212.

Brehony, K.J. (1995) 'Race, ethnicity and racism in the governing of schools', in M.Craft and S.Tomlinson (eds), *Ethnic relations in schools in the 1990s.* London: UCL.Press.

Brighouse, T. (2014) 'Trojan Horse affair: five lessons we must learn', *The Guardian*, 17 June. Available at: http://www.theguardian.com/education/2014/jun/17/trojan-horse-affair-five-lessons-help-schools

Bryson, J.M. (2011) *Strategic planning for public and non-profit organizations: A guide to strengthening and sustaining organizational achievement* (vol 1), London: John Wiley & Sons.

Burton, M. (2014) *The politics of public sector reform: From Thatcher to the Coalition*, London: Palgrave Macmillan.

Bush, T. (ed) (1989) *Managing education: Theory and practice,* Milton Keynes: Open University Press.

Cabinet Office (2011) *Building the Big Society*, London: The Cabinet Office.

Callaghan, J. (1976) 'Ruskin College speech', *Times Educational Supplement*, 22: 72.

Cameron, D. (2010) 'David Cameron's speech in full', *The Guardian*, 11 May. Available at: http://www.theguardian.com/politics/2010/may/11/david-cameron-speech-full-text

Cameron, D. (2011) 'Speech on radicalisation and extremism', Munich Security Conference, Munich. Available at: http://www.newstatesman.com/blogs/the-staggers/2011/02/terrorism-islam-ideology

Campbell-Smith, D. (2008) *Follow the money. The Audit Commission, public money and the management of public services, 1983–2008*, London: Allen Lane.

Caravallo Johnson, G. and Watson, G. (2004) '"Oh Gawd, how am I going to fit into this?": producing mature first-year student identity', *Language and Education*, 18(6): 474–86.

Carey, J.W. (2008) *Communication as culture, revised edition: Essays on media and society*, London: Routledge.

Carmichael, N. and Wild, E. (2012) *Who governs the governors? School governance in the 21st century*, London: Wild Search.

Case, P., Case, S. and Simon, C. (2000) 'Please show you're working: a critical assessment of the impact of OFSTED inspection on primary teachers', *British Journal of Sociology of Education*, 21(4): 605–21.

CfBT (Centre for British Teachers) (2009) *School governors and the new partnership arrangements*, London: Centre for British Teachers.

Chapman, C., Collins, A., Sammons, P., Armstrong, P. and Muijs, D. (2009) 'The impact of federations on student outcomes', Project Report, National College for School Leadership, Nottingham, UK.

Chapman, C., Lindsay, G., Muijs, D., Harris, A., Arweck, E. and Goodall, J. (2010) 'Governance, leadership, and management in federations of schools', *School Effectiveness and School Improvement*, 21(1): 53–74.

Chreim, S., Williams, B.E.B. and Hinings, C.R. (2007) 'Interlevel influences on the reconstruction of professional role identity', *The Academy of Management Journal*, 50(6): 1515–39.

Clarke, J. (2004) *Changing welfare, changing states: New directions in social policy*, London: Sage.

Clarke, J. (2007) 'Citizen-consumers and public service reform: at the limits of neo-liberalism?' *Policy Futures in Education*, 5(2): 239–48.

Clarke, J. (2008) 'Performance paradoxes: the politics of evaluation in public services', in H. Davis and S. Martin (eds) *Public services inspection in the UK*, London: Jessica Kingsley.

Clarke, J. (2009) 'Governance puzzles', in L. Budd and L. Harris (eds) *eGovernance: Managing or governing*, London: Routledge.

Clarke, J. (2011) 'Governing schools at several distances', American Anthropological Association Annual Conference 'Panel on Tracing Policy: Translation and Assemblage', Montreal, Canada, 16–20 November.

Clarke, J. and Newman, J. (1997) *The managerial state: Power, politics and ideology in the remaking of social welfare*, London: Sage.

Clarke, J., Gewirtz, S., Hughes, G. and Humphrey, J. (2000) 'Guarding the public interest? Auditing public services', in J. Clarke, S. Gewirtz and E. McLaughlin (eds) *New managerialism new welfare*, London: Sage.

REFERENCES

Clarke, J., Newman, J., Smith, N., Vidler, E. and Westmarland, L. (2007) *Creating citizen consumers: Changing publics and changing public services*, London: Sage.

Clarke, P. (2014) *Report into allegations concerning Birmingham schools arising from the 'Trojan Horse letter'* (vol HC 756), London: House of Commons, p 124.

Communities.gov.uk (2011) 'Annual Citizenship Survey: April 2010–March 2011, England', 22 September. Available at: http://webarchive.nationalarchives.gov.uk/20120919132719/http:/www.communities.gov.uk/publications/corporate/statistics/citizenshipsurveyq4201011

Converse, P.E. (1964) *Ideology and discontent*, London: Sage.

Cooling, T. (2014) 'The religious are better than Ofsted at policing extremism in schools', *Times Education Supplement*, 2 December. Available at: https://www.tes.co.uk/news/school-news/breaking-views/%E2%80%98-religious-are-better-ofsted-policing-extremism-schools%E2%80%99

Cordingley, P., Bell, M., Rundell, B. and Evans, D. (2005) *The impact of collaborative continuing professional development (CPD) on classroom teaching and learning*, Research Evidence in Education Library, London: EPPI-Centre, Social Science Research Unit, Institute of Education, University of London.

Cornforth, C. (2001) 'Understanding the governance of non-profit organizations: multiple perspectives and paradoxes', 30th Annual ARNOVA Conference, Miami, FL, 29 November–1 December. Available at: http://oro.open.ac.uk/15392/1/ARNOVA_paper_2001.pdf

Cornforth, C. (2004) *The governance of public and non-profit organizations*, London: Routledge.

Cornforth, C. and Edwards, C. (1999) 'Board roles in the strategic management of non-profit organisations: theory and practice', *Corporate Governance: An International Review*, 7(4): 346–62.

Crouch, C. (2003) *Commercialization or citizenship: Education policy and the future of public services*, London: The Fabian Society.

Dale, R. (1981) 'Control, accountability and William Tyndale', *Education and the State*, 2: 305–18.

Davis, J. (2002) 'The Inner London Education Authority and the William Tyndale Junior School affair, 1974–1976', *Oxford Review of Education*, 28(2/3): 275–98.

Deacon, A. (1978) 'The scrounging controversy: public attitudes towards the unemployed in contemporary Britain,' *Social and Economic Administration,* 12(2):120-35.

Dean, C., Dyson, A., Gallannaugh, F., Howes, A. and Raffo, C. (2007) *Schools, governors and disadvantage*, York: Joseph Rowntree Foundation.

Dean, M. (2013) *Democracy under attack: How the media distort policy and politics*, Bristol: Policy Press.

Deem, R. (1990). The reform of school governing bodies: the power of the consumer over the producer?', in M. Flude and M. Hammer (eds), *The 1988 Education Reform Act: Its origins and implications*, London: Falmer Press, pp 153–71..

Deem, R. and Brehony, K. (1994) 'Why didn't you use a survey to generalize your findings? Methodological issues in a multiple site case study of school governing bodies after the 1988 Reform Act', in D. Halpin and B. Troyna (eds) *Researching education policy: Ethical and methodological issues*, London: Falmer.

Deem, R., Brehony, K. and Heath, S. (1995) *Active citizenship and the governing of schools*, Buckingham: Open University Press.

DfE (Department for Education) (2010) *The importance of teaching: The Schools White Paper 2010*, Cm 7980, London: DfE. Available at: https://www.gov.uk/government/publications/the-importance-of-teaching-the-schools-white-paper-2010

DfE (2011a) *Approved free school proposals*, London: DfE. Available at: http://www.education.gov.uk/schools/leadership/typesofschools/freeschools

DfE (2011b) *Research on the role of school governors* (vol 2012), London: DfE.

DfE (2012) *Huge increase in academies takes total to more than 2300*, London: DfE. Available at: https://www.gov.uk/government/news/huge-increase-in-academies-takes-total-to-more-than-2300

DfE (2014a) *Academies/free schools impact indicators 23, 24, 25*, London: DfE.

DfE (2014b) *The governors handbook*, London: DfE.

DfE (2014c) *Guidance on promoting British values in schools published*, London: DfE. Available at: https://www.gov.uk/government/news/guidance-on-promoting-british-values-in-schools-published

DfE (2015a) *Coasting schools: Illustrative regulations*, London: DfE. Available at: https://www.gov.uk/government/publications/coasting-schools-illustrative-regulations

DfE (2015b) *Governance handbook: For trustees of academies and multi-academy trusts and governors of maintained schools*, London: Department for Education.

Dominiczak, P. (2015) 'Every failing school to become an academy', *The Telegraph*, 3 June. Available at: http://www.telegraph.co.uk/education/11647618/Every-failing-school-to-become-an-academy.html

Durose, C., Greasley, S. and Richardson, L. (2009) *Changing local governance, changing citizens*, Bristol: The Policy Press.

EAC-EA (Educational, Audiovisual and Culture Executive Agency) and DG EAC (Directorate General Education and Culture) (2010) *Volunteering in the European Union*, London: GHK Consulting. Available at: http://ec.europa.eu/citizenship/pdf/doc1018_en.pdf

Easton, G. (2009) 'Failing schools to be academies: Gove speech to the Tory Party conference', *BBC News*, 7 October. Available at: http://news.bbc.co.uk/1/hi/education/8294444.stm

Ehren, M. and Swanborn, M.S. (2012) 'Strategic data use of schools in accountability systems', *School Effectiveness and School Improvement*, 23(2): 257–80.

Ehren, M. and Visscher, A. (2008) 'The relationships between school inspections, school characteristics and school improvement', *British Journal of Educational Studies*, 56(2): 205–27.

Entwistle, V. and Sheldon, T. (1999) 'The picture of health? Media coverage of the health service', in B. Franklin (ed) *Social policy, the media and misrepresentation*, London: Routledge.

ESC (Education Select Committee) (2013) *The role of school governing bodies (vols 1–3)*, London: The House of Commons Education Committee.

Esmond, J., Dunlop, P. and Clan, W.A. (2004) *Developing the volunteer motivation inventory to assess the underlying motivational drives of volunteers in Western Australia*, Western Australia: CLAN.

Farrell, C. (2005) 'Governance in the UK public sector: the involvement of the governing board', *Public Administration*, 83(1): 89–110.

Farrell, C., Wohlstetter, P. and Smith, J. (2012) 'Charter management organizations: an emerging approach to scaling up what works', *Educational Policy*, 26(4): 499–532.

Farrell, J.M., Johnston, M.E. and Twynam, G.D. (1998) 'Volunteer motivation, satisfaction, and management at an elite sporting competition', *Journal of Sport Management*, 12(4): 288–300.

Feldman, N. (2012) *The fall and rise of the Islamic State*, Princeton, NJ: Princeton University Press.

Ferrari, N. (2015) 'Schools must stop pupils joining ISIS', LBC Radio, 16 June. Available at: http://www.lbc.co.uk/sir-michael-wilshaw-live-on-lbc-watch-from-9am-111350

Figazzolo, L. (2009) 'Impact of PISA 2006 on the education policy debate', *Education International*. Available at: http://download.ei-ie.org/docs/IRISDocuments/Research%20Website%20Documents/2009-00036-01-E.pdf

Finch, J. (1984) *Education as social policy*, London: Longman.

Fink, J. (2004) *Care: Personal lives and social policy*, Bristol: The Policy Press.

Flinders, M. (2008) *Delegated governance and the British state: Walking without order*, Oxford: Oxford University Press.

Francis, B. (2011) *(Un)Satisfactory: Enhancing life chances by improving 'satisfactory schools'*, London: Royal Society of Arts.

Franklin, B. (2002) *Social policy, the media and misrepresentation*, London: Routledge.

Fujiwara, D., Oroyemi, P. and McKinnon, E. (2013) *Welling and civil society: Estimating the value of volunteering using subjective wellbeing data*, Working Paper 211, London: Department for Work and Pensions and the Cabinet Office.

Garner, R. (2013) 'Derby school Al-Madinah closed after facing accusations of imposing strict Islamic practices', *The Independent*, 2 October. Available at:http://www.independent.co.uk/news/education/education-news/derby-school-almadinah-closed-after-facing-accusations-of-imposing-strict-islamic-practices-8853180.html

Giddens, A. (1984) *The constitution of society*, Cambridge: Polity Press.

REFERENCES

Giddens, A. (1991) *Modernity and self-identity*, Cambridge, MA: Polity Press.

Glatter, R., Bagley, C. and Woods, P. (1997) *Choice and diversity in schooling: Perspectives and prospects*, London: Routledge.

Goffman, E. (1959) *The presentation of self in everyday life*, London: Penguin.

Goffman, E. (1974a) *Frame analysis*, New York, NY: Harper and Row.

Goffman, E. (1974b) *Frame analysis: An essay on the organization of experience*, Harvard, MA: Harvard University Press.

Goffman, E. (1981) *Forms of talk*, Pennsylvania, PA: University of Pennsylvania Press.

Goffman, E. (2008) *Behavior in public places*, New York, NY: Simon and Schuster.

Goffman, E. (2009) *Relations in public*, London: Transaction Publishers.

Golding, P. and Middleton, S. (1982) *Images of welfare: Press and public attitudes to poverty*, Oxford: Robertson.

Gorard, S. (1999) 'Well. That about wraps it up for school choice research': a state of the art review, *School Leadership and Management*, 19(1): 25–47.

Gove, M. (2006) *Celsius 7/7: How the West's policy of appeasement has provoked yet more fundamentalist terror – and what has to be done now*, London: Phoenix.

Gov.uk (2011) 'Prevent Strategy 2011'. Available at: www.gov.uk/government/publications/prevent-strategy-2011

Gov.uk (2015) *Extremism in schools: the Trojan Horse affair. Seventh report of session 2014–15* (HC473), London. Available at: http://www.publications.parliament.uk/pa/cm201415/cmselect/cmeduc/473/473.pdf

Green, D. (2014) 'Ofsted vs English education', *The Spectator*, 26 January. Available at: http://blogs.spectator.co.uk/coffeehouse/2014/01/ofsted-vs-english-education/

Grek, S. (2008) *PISA in the British media: Leaning tower or robust testing tool?*, University of Edinburgh: CES.

Grek, S. (2009) 'Governing by numbers: the PISA 'effect' in Europe', *Journal of Education Policy*, 24(1): 23–37.

Grek, S. and Lindgren, J. (eds) (2014) *Governing by inspection*, London: Routledge.

Griffiths, S., Kerbaj, R. and Graham, G. (2013) 'Pupils ordered to wear hijab out of school', *The Sunday Times*, 29 September. Available at: http://www.thesundaytimes.co.uk/sto/news/uk_news/Society/article1320580.ece

Gunter, H.M. (2011) *The state and education policy: The academies programme*, London: Bloomsbury Publishing.

Hajer, M.A. (1993) 'Discourse coalitions and the institutionalization of practice: the case of acid rain in Great Britain', in F. Fishcher and J. Forester (eds) *The argumentative turn in policy analysis and planning*, Durham, NC: Duke University Press.

Hajer, M.A. (1995) *The politics of environmental discourse*, Oxford: Oxford University Press.

Hajer, M.A. (2009) *Authoritative governance: Policy making in the age of mediatization*, Oxford: Oxford University Press.

Hall, S. (1995) 'Fantasy, identity, politics', in E. Carter, J. Donald and J. Squires (eds) *Cultural remix: Theories of politics and the popular*, London: Lawrence and Wishart.

Hall, S. (1996) 'Who needs identity?', *Questions of Cultural Identity*, 16(2): 1–17.

Hall, S. (1997) *Representation: Cultural representations and signifying practices* (vol 2), London: Sage.

Hall, S., Critcher, C., Jefferson, T., Clarke, J. and Roberts, B. (1978) *Policing the crisis: Mugging, the state, and law and order*, London: Macmillan.

Halstead, J.M. and Taylor, M.J. (2000) 'Learning and teaching about values: a review of recent research', *Cambridge Journal of Education*, 30(2): 169–202.

Harris, M. and Rochester, C. (2001) *Voluntary organisations and social policy in Britain: Perspectives on change and choice*, London: Palgrave Macmillan.

Harrison, D.A. (1995) 'Volunteer motivation and attendance decisions: competitive theory testing in multiple samples from a homeless shelter', *Journal of Applied Psychology*, 80(3): 371.

Harvey, D. (2005) *A brief history of neoliberalism*, Oxford: Oxford University Press.

Hatcher, R. (1994) 'Market relationships and the management of teachers', *British Journal of Sociology of Education*, 15(1): 41–61.

Hatcher, R. (2006) 'Privatization and sponsorship: the re-agenting of the school system in England 1', *Journal of Education Policy*, 21(5): 599–619.

Hatcher, R. and Jones, K. (2011) *No country for the young: Education from New Labour to the Coalition*, London: Tufnell Press.

HCEC (House of Commons Education Committee) (2014–15) *House of Commons Education Committee: Academies and free schools*, London: House of Commons Education Committee.

Henderson, A. (ed) (2011) *Insights from the Playgroup Movement: Equality and autonomy in a voluntary organization*, Stoke on Trent: Trentham Books.

Hibbert, S., Piacentini, M. and Dajani, H.A. (2003) 'Understanding volunteer motivation for participation in a community-based food cooperative', *International Journal of Nonprofit and Voluntary Sector Marketing*, 8(1): 30–42.

Higham, R. and Hopkins, D. (2007) 'System leadership for educational renewal in England: the case of federations and executive heads', *Australian Journal of Education*, 51(3): 299.

Hiro, D. (2013) *Holy wars*, London: Routledge.

HM Government (2011) *Prevent Strategy*. London: The Stationery Office.

Home Office (1967) *The place of voluntary service after-care: Second report of the working party,* HMSO: London. [Reading Committee].

Home Office (1978) *The Government and the Voluntary Sector: A consultative document,* Voluntary Services Unit, Home Office: London.

Hossein, N., Dagli, C.K., Massi, M.D., Lumbard, J.E.B. and Rustom, M. (2015) *The study Quran: A new translation and commentary*, Italy: Harper Collins.

Hough, A., McGregor-Lowndes, M. and Ryan, C. (2014) 'Board monitoring and judgement as processes of sensemaking', in C. Cornforth and W.A. Brown (eds) *Nonprofit governance*, London: Routledge, pp 142–59.

Husserl, E. (1997) *Collected works: Psychological and transcendental phenomenology and the confrontation with Heidegger (1927–1931)* (vol 6), Berlin: Kluwer Academic Publishers.

Institute for Volunteering Research (2015) 'How has the number of people volunteering changed over time?', 8 September. Available at: http://www.ivr.org.uk/ivr-volunteering-stats/174-how-has-number-of-people-volunteering-changed

International Centre for the Study of Radicalisation (2015) 'International Centre for the Study of Radicalisation'. Available at: http://www.kcl.ac.uk/sspp/departments/warstudies/research/groups/icsr.aspx

James, C., Brammer, S., Connolly, M., Fertig, M., James, J. and Jones, J. (2011) 'School governing bodies in England under pressure: the effects of socio-economic context and school performance', *Educational Management Administration & Leadership*, 39(4): 414–33.

James, C., Brammer, S., Connolly, M., Fertig, M., James, J. and Jones, J. (2012) *The hidden givers: A study of school governing bodies in England*, Bath: The University of Bath.

James, C., Brammer, S., Connolly, M., Spicer, D.E., James, J. and Jones, J. (2013) 'The challenges facing school governing bodies in England: a "perfect storm"?', *Management in Education*, 27(3): 84–90.

James, C., Goodall, J., Howarth, E. and Knights, E. (2014) *The state of school governing in England 2014*, Birmingham: NGA and The University of Bath.

John, P. (2009) 'Citizen governance: where it came from, where it's going', in C. Durose, S. Greasley and L. Richardson (eds) *Changing local governance, changing citizens*, Bristol: The Policy Press.

Jones, K. (2003) *Education in Britain: 1944 to the present*, Cambridge: Polity Press.

Kendall, J. and Knapp, M. (1996) *The voluntary sector in the UK*, Manchester: Manchester University Press.

Kerbaj, R. and Griffiths, S. (2014) 'Islamist plot to take over schools', *The Sunday Times*, 2 March, pp 22–30.

Kershaw, I. (2014) *Investigation report: Trojan Horse letter*, Birmingham: Northern Education.

Key for School Governors (2015) 'The role of school governors, survey'. Available at: https://www.thekeysupport.com/media/filer_public/cc/77/cc77c169-381e-4aee-9515-a279928d4917/schools_today_-_the_governor_perspective_web.pdf

King, D. (1987) *The New Right: Politics, markets and citizenship*, Basingstoke: Macmillan.

Kingdon, J.W. and Thurber, J.A. (1984) *Agendas, alternatives, and public policies* (vol 45), Boston, MA: Little, Brown.

Klees, S., Samoff, J. and Stromquist, N. (2012) *The World Bank and education*, The Netherlands: Sense.

Knights, E. (2014) 'The Trojan Horse review', National Governors' Association. Available at: http://www.nga.org.uk/News/NGA-News/May-Sept-14/Trojan-Horse-Review.aspx

Knights, E. (2015) 'NGA responds to HMCI's commentary on the importance of governance'. Available at: http://www.nga.org.uk/News/NGA-News/NGA-responds-to-HMCI%E2%80%99s-commentary-on-the-importanc.aspx

Kooiman, J. (2003) *Governing as governance*, London: Sage.

Lakoff, G. and Johnson, M. (1999) *Philosophy in the flesh*, New York, NY: Basic Books.

Lawn, M. (2013) 'A systemless system: designing the disarticulation of English state education', *European Educational Research Journal*, 12(2): 231–41.

Lawn, M., Baxter, J., Segerholm, C. and Grek, S. (2014) 'Inspection and the local', in S. Grek and J. Lindgren (eds) *Governing by inspection*, London: Routledge.

Lawson, N. (1992) *The view from No. 11. Memoirs of a Tory radical*, London: Bantam and Cheltenham: Edward Elgar Publishing.

Lawton, D. (1979) *End of the 'secret garden'? Study in the politics of the curriculum. An inaugural lecture by Professor Denis Lawton*, London: Institute of Education, University of London.

Lawton, D. (1994) *The Tory mind on education 1979–94*, London: The Falmer Press.

Lawton, D. (2005) *Education and the Labour Party ideologies: 1900–2001 and beyond*, Oxford: Routledge Falmer.

Lawton, D. and Gordon, P. (1987) *HMI*, London: Routledge.

Lepkowska, D. (2012) 'The first "outstanding" school of 2012 reveals all', *The Guardian*, 13 February. Available at: http://www.theguardian.com/education/2012/feb/13/outstanding-osted-for-birmingham-school

Leveson, Lord Justice (2012) 'The Leveson Inquiry: culture, practice and ethics of the press'. Available at: https://www.gov.uk/government/publications/leveson-inquiry-report-into-the-culture-practices-and-ethics-of-the-press

Lewis, D. (2012) 'The Big Society and social policy', in A. Ishkanian and S. Szreter (eds) *The Big Society debate: A new agenda for social welfare?*, Cheltenham: Edward Elgar Publishing.

Lindsay, G., Muijs, D., Harris, A., Chapman, C., Arweck, E. and Goodall, J. (2007) *School federations pilot study 2003–2007*, Research Report DCSF-RR015, Warwick: University of Warwick.

Lingard, B. and Rawolle, S. (2004) 'Mediatizing educational policy: the journalistic field, science policy, and cross-field effects', *Journal of Education Policy*, 19(3): 361–80.

Lowe, R. (2002) 'A century of local education authorities: what has been lost?', *Oxford Review of Education*, 28(2/3): 149–58.

Lundby, K. (ed) (2009) *Mediatization. Concept, changes, consequences*, New York, NY: Peter Lang.

Maclure, S. (1989) *Education re-formed: A guide to the Education Reform Act*, London: Hodder & Stoughton.

Maclure, S. (2000) *The inspectors' calling*, Oxford: Hodder & Stoughton.

Macmillan, R. (2011) 'Supporting the voluntary sector in an age of austerity: the UK Coalition government's consultation on improving support for frontline civil society organisations in England', *Voluntary Sector Review*, 2(1): 115–24.

Maguire, K. and Truscott, F. (2006) 'Active governance: The value added by community involvement in governance through local strategic partnerships'. Available at: https://www.jrf.org.uk/report/value-added-community-involvement-governance

Mair, P. (2013) *Ruling the void: The hollowing out of Western democracy*, London: Verso.

Major, J. (1991) 'Education: all our futures', Speech to the Centre for Policy Studies, Café Royale, London, 3 July.

Major, J. (2000) *John Major: The autobiography* (Kindle version), London: HarperCollins.

Mansell, W. (2009) 'Education: who's in charge here? A new report warns that school governors, traditionally amateurs holding professionals to account, are becoming powerless "pawns". Does it matter?' *The Guardian, Education*, 10 November, p 1.

Marshall, T.H. (1964) *Class, citizenship and social development*, New York, NY: Doubleday and Co.

Mason, R. (2014) 'Nicky Morgan completes rapid rise to Cameron's top team', *The Guardian*, 15 July. Available at: http://www.theguardian.com/politics/2014/jul/15/nicky-morgan-education-secretary-women-cameron

Matthews, P. (2009) *Twelve outstanding secondary schools: Excelling against the odds,* London, Ofsted.

Matthews, P. and Sammons, P. (2004) 'Improvement through inspection: an evaluation of the impact of Ofsted's work', July. Available at: http://dera.ioe.ac.uk/4969/3/3696.pdf

Matthias, C. (2014) *National leaders of governance study*, London: NCTL.

Maw, J. (1995) 'The handbook for the inspection of schools: a critique', *Cambridge Journal of Education*, 25(1): 75–87.

McCrone, T., Southcott, C. and George, N. (2011) *Governance models in schools*, London: NFER.

McKendrick, J.H., Sinclair, S., Irwin, A., O'Donnell, H., Scott, G. and Dobbie, L. (2008) *The media, poverty and public opinion in the UK*, London: Joseph Rowntree Foundation.

Meegan, R., Kennett, P., Jones, G. and Croft, J. (2014) 'Global economic crisis, austerity and neoliberal urban governance in England', *Cambridge Journal of Regions, Economy and Society*, 7(1): 137–53.

Mohan, J. (2011) *Mapping the Big Society: Perspectives from the third sector research centre*, London: The Third Sector Research Centre.

Moore, C. (2014) 'The Trojan Horse affair proves Michael Gove right – and MI5 wrong', *The Spectator*, 26 July. Available at: http://www.spectator.co.uk/columnists/the-spectators-notes/9271001/the-spectators-notes-388/

Morey, P. and Yaqin, A. (2011) *Framing Muslims*, Cambridge: Harvard University Press.

Morgan, N. (2014) 'Nicky Morgan: "Trojan Horse report findings 'disturbing'"', video, *The Guardian*, 22 July. Available at: http://www.theguardian.com/education/video/2014/jul/22/nicky-morgan-trojan-horse-report-birmingham-schools-video

Morris, J. and Farrell, C. (2007) 'The "post-bureaucratic" public sector organization. New organizational forms and HRM in ten UK public sector organizations', *The International Journal of Human Resource Management*, 18(9): 1575–88.

Nakano, L.Y. (2000) 'Volunteering as a lifestyle choice: negotiating self-identities in Japan', *Ethnology*, 39(2): 93–107.

NCTL (National College for Teaching and Leadership) (2013) *Governance in multi academy trusts*, London: National College for Teaching and Leadership.

Neely, A.D. (2002) *Business performance measurement: Theory and practice*, Cambridge: Cambridge University Press.

Negrine, R. (2013) *Politics and the mass media in Britain*, London: Routledge.

Newman, J. (2001) *Modernising governance: New Labour, policy and society*, London: Sage.

Newman, J. and Clarke, J. (2009) *Publics, politics and power: Remaking the public in public services*, London: Sage.

NGA (National Governors' Association) (2010) *What governing bodies should expect from school leaders and what school leaders should expect from governing bodies*, London: National Governors' Association. Available at: www.nga.org

Nias, J. (1981) 'Commitment and motivation in primary school teachers', *Educational Review*, 33(3): 181–90.

Nye, P. (2015) *Regional schools commissioners. Your guide to who, what and where*, London: Schools Week.

OECD (Organisation for Economic Co-operation and Development) (2010a) 'PISA 2009 results. What students know and can do', in OECD (ed) *OECD 50*, Paris: OECD. Available at: http://www.oecd.org/pisa/pisaproducts/48852548.pdf

OECD (2010b) *Viewing the United Kingdom school system through the prism of PISA*, Paris: OECD. Available at: http://www.oecd.org/pisa/46624007.pdf

OECD (2011) 'Governing complex education systems' available at: http://www.oecd.org/edu/ceri/governingcomplexeducationsystemsgces.htm

OECD (2015) *OECD better policies for better lives*, Paris: OECD. Available at: http://www.oecd.org/pisa/aboutpisa/

Ofsted (Office for Standards in Education, Children's Services and Skills) (1993) *Framework for the inspection of schools*, London: Ofsted.

Ofsted (1994) *The consolidated handbook for the inspection of schools*, London: Ofsted.

Ofsted (1995) *Handbook for the inspection of schools*, London: HMSO.

Ofsted (2002) *The work of governors: 1999–2001*, London: Ofsted.

Ofsted (2004) *The future of school inspection: New inspections and the viewpoint of users*, London: Ofsted.

Ofsted (2008) *Using data, improving schools*, London: Ofsted.

Ofsted (2009) *The framework for school inspection in England under section 5 of the Education Act 2005, from September 2009*, London: Ofsted.

Ofsted (2011a) 'Good governance essential to school improvement'. Available at: http://www.wired-gov.net/wg/wg-news-1.nsf/0/5D D61106101CD79B80257894002D3A84?OpenDocument

Ofsted (2011b) *Leadership of more than one school: An evaluation of the impact of federated schools*, London: Ofsted.

Ofsted (2011c) 'School governance: learning from the best'. Available at: https://www.essex.gov.uk/Business-Partners/ Partners/Schools/school-governors/Monitoring-and-evaluation/ Documents/Ofsted%20Report%20Summary%20-%20School%20 governance[1].pdf

Ofsted (2012) *The framework for school inspection, January 2012*, London: Ofsted.

Ofsted (2013a) 'Chief Inspector raises the stakes for school governance', *Ofsted News*, 27 February. Available at: http://www.ofsted.gov.uk/ news/chief-inspector-raises-stakes-for-school-governance

Ofsted (2013b) 'Data view: regional breakdown'. Available at: http:// www.ofsted.gov.uk

Ofsted (2013c) 'Ofsted report on Al-Madinah school in Derby', *The Guardian*, 16 October. Available at: http://www.theguardian.com/ education/interactive/2013/oct/16/oftsed-report-on-al-madinah-school-derby

Ofsted (2014) *The school inspection handbook (July 2014 for use from September 2014)*, London: Ofsted.

Ofsted (2015) *The school inspection handbook from September 2015*, London: Ofsted.

Ofsted (2015a) *Better inspection for all: A report on the responses to the consultation*, London: Ofsted.

Ofsted (2015b) *The future of education inspection: Understanding the changes*, London: Ofsted.

Ofsted (2015c) 'Supplementary evidence submitted by Ofsted'. Available at: http://data.parliament.uk/writtenevidence/committeeevidence. svc/evidencedocument/education-committee/the-role-of-regional-schools-commissioners/written/25050.pdf

Opfer, V.D. (2007) 'Developing a research agenda on the media and education', *Peabody Journal of Education*, 82(1): 166–77.

Oppenheim, C. and Lister, R. (1997) 'The growth of poverty and inequality', in A. Walker and C. Walker (eds) *Britain divided: The growth of social exclusion in the 1980s and 1990s*, London: Child Poverty Action Group, pp 17–31.

Ozga, J. (2009) 'Governing education through data in England: from regulation to self-evaluation', *Journal of Education Policy*, 24(2): 149–62.

Ozga, J., Dahler-Larsen, P., Segerholm, C. and Simola, H. (2011) *Fabricating quality in education: Data and governance in Europe*, London: Routledge.

Ozga, J., Baxter, J., Clarke, J., Grek, S. and Lawn, M. (2013) 'The politics of educational change: governance and school inspection in England and Scotland', *Swiss Journal of Sociology*, 39(2): 37–55.

Panjwani, F. (2014) 'Beyond the saga of the "Trojan Horse": some reflections on teaching about Islam in schools', *The Middle East in London*, 10(5): 9–15.

Parekh, B. (2000) *The future of multi-ethnic Britain: The Commission on the Future of Multi-Ethnic Britain*, London: The Runnymede Trust.

Parliament (1944) *The Education Act 1944*, London: HMSO. Available at: http://www.parliament.uk/about/living-heritage/transformingsociety/livinglearning/school/overview/educationact1944/

Parliament (1977) *The Taylor report*, London: HMSO. Available at: http://www.educationengland.org.uk/documents/taylor/

Parliament (1997) *The Mountfield Report,* London: HMSO. Available at: http://www.parliament.the-stationery-office.co.uk/pa/cm199798/cmselect/cmpubadm/770/77006.htm

Parliament (2010a) *The Phillis Review,* 'Chapter 2: Events that led to the Phillis Review', London: HMSO. Available at: http://www.publications.parliament.uk/pa/ld200809/ldselect/ldcomuni/7/704.htm

Parliament (2010b) *Spending review*, London: HM Treasury.

Parliament (2012) *All Party Parliamentary Group on Education Governance and Leadership*, London: HMSO

Parliament (2013a) *The role of school governing bodies: Second report of session 2013–14, volume III*, London: HMSO.

Parliament (2013b) *The role of school governing bodies: Second report of session 2013–14, volume II*, London: The House of Commons.

Parliament (2013c) *The role of school governing bodies: Second report of session 2013–14, volume I*, London: House of Commons Education Committee.

Parliament (2014) *Extremism in Schools: The Trojan Horse Affair: Education Seventh Report*, London: House of Commons Education Committee: Available at: http://www.publications.parliament.uk/pa/cm201415/cmselect/cmeduc/473/47308.htm

Parliament (2016) *Report: The role of Regional Schools Commissioners:* London: House of Commons Education Committee. Available at: http://www.parliament.uk/business/committees/committees-a-z/commons-select/education-committee/news-parliament-2015/regional-schools-report-published-15-16/

Paton, G. (2012) 'Ofsted: one million children stuck in coasting schools', *The Telegraph*, 1 February. Available at: http://www.telegraph.co.uk/education/educationnews/9020744/Ofsted-one-million-children-stuck-in-coasting-schools.html

Paton, G. (2013) 'Sack the worst performing school governors, say MPs', *The Telegraph*, 4 July. Available at: http://www.telegraph.co.uk/education/educationnews/10157657/Sack-the-worst-performing-school-governors-say-MPs.html

Patriotta, G. (2003) 'Sensemaking on the shop floor: narratives of knowledge in organizations', *Journal of Management Studies*, 40(2): 349–75.

Perry, A., Amadeo, C., Fletcher, M. and Walker, E. (2010) *Instinct or reason: How education policy is made and how we might make it better*, London: CfBT.

Perry, E. and Francis, B. (2010) *The social class gap for educational achievement*, London: Royal Society of Arts.

Petley, J. (2013) *Pointing the finger: Islam and Muslims in the British media*, London: Oneworld Publications.

Phillis, R. (2004) *An independent review of government communications*, London: The Cabinet Office.

Pierre, J. and Peters, B.G. (2000) *Governance, politics and the state*, Basingstoke: Macmillan.

Plowden, B. (1967) *The Plowden report: Children and their primary schools*, London: CACE.

Pons, X. (2011) 'What do we really learn from PISA? The sociology of its reception in three European countries (2001–2008) 1', *European Journal of Education*, 46(4): 540–8.

Power, M. (1994) *The audit explosion*, London: Demos.

Power, M. (1997a) *The audit society*, Oxford: Oxford University Press.

Power, M. (1997b) *The audit society: Rituals of verification*, Oxford: Oxford University Press.

Prokhovnik, R. (2005) *Making policy, shaping lives*, Edinburgh: Edinburgh University Press.

Raab, C. (1993) 'Education and the impact of the New Right', in G. Jordan and N. Ashford (eds) *Public policy and the impact of the New Right*, London: Pinter.

Ranson, S. (2003) 'Public accountability in the age of neo-liberal governance', in B. Lingard, S. Rawolle, S. Taylor and J. Ozga (eds) *The Routledge Falmer reader in education policy and politics*, London: Routledge, pp 198–220.

Ranson, S. and Crouch, C. (2009) *Towards a new governance of schools in the re-making of civil society*, Warwick: Institute of Education, University of Warwick.

Ranson, S., Arnott, M., McKeown, P., Martin, J. and Smith, P. (2005) 'The participation of volunteer citizens in school governance', *Educational Review*, 57(3): 357–71.

Rawolle, S. (2007) 'When the knowledge economy became the chance to change mediatization, cross-field effects and temporary social fields'. Available at: http://espace.library.uq.edu.au/view/UQ:138898

Rayner, S. (2003) 'Democracy in the age of assessment: reflections on the roles of expertise and democracy in public-sector decision making', *Science and Public Policy*, 30(3): 163–70.

Reeve, J.M. (1992) *Understanding motivation and emotion*, Fort Worth, TX: Harcourt Brace Jovanovich.

Reunanen, E., Kunelius, R. and Noppari, E. (2010) 'Mediatization in context: consensus culture, media and decision making in the 21st century, the case of Finland', *Communications*, 35(3): 287–307.

Richardson, R. (2015) 'British values and British identity: muddles, mixtures and ways ahead', *London Review of Education*, 13(2): 37–47.

Roberts, A., Marshall, L. and Charlesworth, A. (2012) *A decade of austerity? The funding pressures facing the NHS from 2010/11 to 2021/22*, London: Nuffield Trust.

Roche, M. (2014) 'Le noyautage d'écoles publiques à Birmingham par des islamistes provoque un scandale politique', 10 June. Available at: www.lemonde.fr/europe/article/2014/06/10/le-noyautage-de-six-ecoles-de-birmingham-par-des-islamistes-provoque-un-scandale-politique_4435459_3214.html#bf7WtIsJTFroz70f.99

Rochester, C., Ellis Paine, A. and Howlett, S. (2012) *Volunteering and society in the 21st century*: London: Palgrave Macmillan.

Roy, O. (2008) 'Al Quaeda in the West as a youth movement: the power of a narrative' Available at: http://www.microconflict.eu/publications/PWP2_OR.pdf

Rustin, S. (2015) 'Should schools teach British values? Ask the Quakers'. Available at: http://www.theguardian.com/education/2015/feb/18/schools-teach-british-values-quakers

Sallis, J. (1988) *Schools, parents and governors: A new approach to accountability*, London: Routledge.

Scheurich, J.J. and Skrla, L. (2004) *Educational equity and accountability: Paradigms, policies and politics*, New York::Routledge Falmer

Schütz, A. (1967) *The phenomenology of the social world*, Illinois, IL: Northwestern University Press.

Seager, A. and Milner, M. (2009) 'Lights go out across Britain as recession hits home', *The Guardian*, 24 January. Available at: http://www.theguardian.com/business/2009/jan/24/recession-britain

Seddon, J. (2008) *Systems thinking in the public sector*, Axminster: Triarchy Press.

Sharp, P. (2002) 'Surviving, not thriving: LEAs since the Education Reform Act of 1988', *Oxford Review of Education*, 28(2/3): 197–215.

Sherwood, H., Laville, S., Wilsher, K., Knight, B., French, M. and Gambino, L. (2014) 'Schoolgirl jihadis: the female Islamists leaving home to join Isis fighters', *The Guardian*, 31 July. Available at: http://www.theguardian.com/world/2014/sep/29/schoolgirl-jihadis-female-islamists-leaving-home-join-isis-iraq-syria

Sinclair, S. (2012) 'National identity and the politics of the "headscarf debate" in Germany', *Culture and Religion*, 13(1): 19–39.

Sinclair, S. (2013) 'More than just a piece of cloth: the German "headscarf" debate', *Implicit Religion, Special Issue on 'Veiling'*, 43(4): 19–39.

Singer, J.B. and Ashman, I. (2009) '"Comment is free, but facts are sacred": user-generated content and ethical constructs at *The Guardian*', *Journal of Mass Media Ethics*, 24(1): 3–21.

Slay, H.S. and Smith, D.A. (2011) 'Professional identity construction: using narrative to understand the negotiation of professional and stigmatized cultural identities', *Human Relations*, 64(1): 85.

Spitzer, R.J. (1993) *Media and public policy*, Santa Barbara, CA: Praeger Publishers.

Stenvall, K. (1993) 'Public policy planning and the problem of governance: the question of education in Finland', in J. Kooiman (ed) *Modern governance*, London: Sage.

Stevenson, H. (2014) 'Some thoughts on "Ofsted wars"', blog, 3 February. Available at: http://howardstevenson.org/2014/02/03/some-thoughts-on-ofsted-wars/

Strömbäck, J. (2008) 'Four phases of mediatization: an analysis of the mediatization of politics', *The International Journal of Press/Politics*, 13(3): 228–46.

Sun, H., Creemers, B.P.M. and De Jong, R. (2007) 'Contextual factors and effective school improvement', *School Effectiveness and School Improvement,* 18(1): 93-122.

The Guardian (2014) 'Ofsted credibility at stake over Trojan Horse schools inquiry'. Available at: http://www.theguardian.com/education/2014/jun/03/ofsted-credibility-at-stake-trojan-horse

Thody, A. (1994) *School governors: Leaders or followers?*, London: Longman.

Thomas, S. (2005) *Education policy in the media: Public discourses on education*, Teneriffe, QLD: Post Pressed.

Trojan Horse Review Group (2014) 'Report to leader of Birmingham City Council', 18 July. Available at: www.birmingham.gov.uk

Van Aelst, P., Thesen, G., Walgrave, S. and Vliegenthart, R. (2013) 'Mediatization and the media's political agenda-setting influence', CAP Conference, Antwerp, Belgium, 27–29 June. Available at: http://euagendas.weebly.com/6th-cap-conference-antwerp.html

Vogler, C. (2007) *The writer's journey: Mythic structure for writers*, Studio City, CA: Michael Wiese Productions.

Volunteering England (2009) 'National statistics'. Available at: http://www.volunteering.org.uk/images/stories/Volunteering-England/Documents/Free-Information-Sheets/IS---National-Statistics--%28VE09%29.pdf?phpMyAdmin=ea19469af65d57852a6dcf96ae252f42&phpMyAdmin=af59e0793933f8849c29e6a3a0aa550d&phpMyAdmin=aOV51K4pN6n2U-SVePLZzBRWAjd

Wallace, M. (1994) 'The contribution of the mass media to the education policy process', *International Journal of Educational Reform*, 4(2): 124–30.

Wallace, M. (1997) 'Guided by an unseen hand: the mass media and education policy', in K. Watson, C. Modgil and S. Modgil (eds) *Educational dilemmas: Debate and diversity: Vol. 3 power and responsibility in education*, London: Cassell, p 147.

Watt, N. and Adams, R. (2014) 'Gove accused of using National Security Council to promote "neocon" ideas', *The Guardian*, 4 June. Available at: http://www.theguardian.com/politics/2014/jun/04/michael-gove-national-security-council-neocon-ideas-theresa-may

Weal, S. (2015) 'Teachers urged to "disengage" from promotion of British values', *The Guardian*, 30 March. Available at: http://www.theguardian.com/politics/2015/mar/30/teachers-urged-to-disengage-from-promotion-of-british-values

Weick, K. (2001) *Making sense of the organization*, London: Blackwell.

Weick, K., Sutcliffe, K.M. and Obstfeld, D. (2005) 'Organizing and the process of sensemaking', *Organization Science*, 16(4): 409–21.

Wells, A.S., Slayton, J. and Scott, J. (2002) 'Defining democracy in the neoliberal age: charter school reform and educational consumption', *American Educational Research Journal*, 39(2): 337–61.

Wenger, E. (1998) *Communities of practice: Learning, meaning, and identity*, New York, NY: Cambridge University Press.

Wilborg, S. (2010) *Swedish free schools: Do they work?*, London: Centre for Learning and Life Chances in Knowledge Economies and Society/The Institute of Education.

Wilkins, A. (2014) 'Professionalizing school governance: the disciplinary effects of school autonomy and inspection on the changing role of school governors', *Journal of Education Policy* (pre-print): 1–19.

Williams, K. (2010) *Read all about it! A history of the British newspaper,* London: Routledge.

Wilshaw, M. (2011) 'Good schools for all – an impossible dream?', speech by Sir Michael Wilshaw, Director of Education, ARK Schools, 29 November. Available at: http://arkonline.org/news/lecture-sir-michael-wilshaw

Wilshaw, M. (2012) 'Strong governance: learning from the best', National Governors' Association Conference, London, 16 June.

Wilshaw, M. (2015a) *21st century governance needed for 21st century schools*, London: Ofsted. Available at: https://www.gov.uk/government/speeches/hmcis-monthly-commentary-november-2015

Wilshaw, M. (2015b) *Advice letter from Sir Michael Wilshaw, Her Majesty's Chief Inspector, on the latest position with schools in Birmingham and Tower Hamlets*, London: Ofsted.

Wohlstetter, P., Smyer, R. and Mohrman, S.A. (1994) 'New boundaries for school-based management: the high involvement model', *Educational Evaluation and Policy Analysis*, 16(3): 268–86.

Wohlstetter, P., Malloy, C.L., Chau, D. and Polhemus, J. (2003) 'Improving schools through networks: a new approach to urban school reform', *Educational Policy*, 17(4): 339–430.

Woods, D. and Brighouse, T. (eds) (2014) *The story of the London Challenge – the London leadership strategy*, London: London ED.

Wright, T., and Gamble, A. (2000).'Commentary: The end of Britain?'. *The Political Quarterly*, 71(1), 1-3.

Yanovitzky, I. (2002) 'Effects of news coverage on policy attention and actions: a closer look into the media–policy connection', *Communication Research*, 29(4): 422–51.

Zaller, J. (1992) *The nature and origins of mass opinion*, Cambridge: Cambridge University Press.

Index